LANGUAGE AND REALITY

A Univocal Book

Drew Burk, Consulting Editor

Univocal Publishing was founded by Jason Wagner and Drew Burk as an independent publishing house specializing in artisanal editions and translations of texts spanning the areas of cultural theory, media archaeology, continental philosophy, aesthetics, anthropology, and more. In May 2017, Univocal ceased operations as an independent publishing house and became a series with its publishing partner, the University of Minnesota Press.

Univocal authors include:

Miguel Abensour
Judith Balso
Jean Baudrillard
Philippe Beck
Simon Critchley
Fernand Deligny
Jacques Derrida
Vinciane Despret
Georges Didi-Huberman
Jean Epstein
Vilém Flusser
Barbara Glowczewski
Evelyne Grossman
Félix Guattari
David Lapoujade
François Laruelle

David Link
Sylvère Lotringer
Jean Malaurie
Michael Marder
Quentin Meillassoux
Friedrich Nietzsche
Peter Pál Pelbart
Jacques Rancière
Lionel Ruffel
Michel Serres
Gilbert Simondon
Étienne Souriau
Isabelle Stengers
Eugene Thacker
Siegfried Zielinski

LANGUAGE AND REALITY

VILÉM FLUSSER

Translated by
Rodrigo Maltez Novaes

Flusser Archive Collection

A Univocal Book

University of Minnesota Press
Minneapolis · London

Published by the University of Minnesota Press
111 Third Avenue South, Suite 290
Minneapolis, MN 55401-2520
http://www.upress.umn.edu

ISBN 978-1-5179-0-4289

A Cataloging-in-Publication record for this book is available from the
Library of Congress.

Printed in the United States of America on acid-free paper
The University of Minnesota is an equal-opportunity educator and
employer.

23 22 21 20 19 18   10 9 8 7 6 5 4 3 2 1

UXORI DILECTISSIMAE

CONTENTS

FLUSSER ARCHIVE COLLECTION

Vilém Flusser is one of the most influential thinkers of the second half of the twentieth century on media and cultural theory and on the philosophy of communication. But unlike certain thinkers on media culture, such as Marshall McLuhan or Jean Baudrillard, most of Flusser's work has yet to gain the proper attention of the reading public inside and outside the walls of the academy. One of the reasons for this is the singular process by which Flusser constructed his thinking and writing. He is a rare polyglot who would write his texts in various languages until he was satisfied with the outcome. Fluent in Czech, German, French, English, and Portuguese, he has left an archive full of thousands of manuscripts in various languages. The Flusser Archive Collection will be a monumental step forward in finally providing an Anglophone readership with a collection of some of Flusser's most important works.

Translator's
Note

The book you have before you is perhaps the most emblematic work from Vilém Flusser's earliest stage of philosophical explorations into language and thought, and it certainly provides a unique lens on Flusser's style of thinking in relation to his own polyglotism. The ten years from 1957 to 1967 marked Flusser's first intense phase of creative production. During this time, he began writing essays for the Brazilian newspaper *O Estado de São Paulo* and taught courses for the Brazilian Institute of Philosophy and the Institute of Technology for Aeronautics. It was also during this period that Flusser published his first series of books. Although not the first book he ever wrote, *Language and Reality* (1963) was the first book that Flusser eventually published. Out of the first two monographs Flusser wrote before writing *Language and Reality,* only *The History of the Devil* would eventually find its way to publication, in 1965.[1] The first monograph that Flusser wrote, titled *The Twentieth Century* (1957), still remains unpublished to this day.

   Language and Reality is thus one of Flusser's main titles from his early period, when he was developing his philosophical project, and as such, it is an important work for understanding his later

---

1 Vilém Flusser, *The History of the Devil,* trans. Rodrigo Maltez Novaes (Minneapolis, Minn.: Univocal, 2014).

periods of thinking. Differently from some of his other works, Flusser chose to write *Language and Reality* strictly in Portuguese, which he used as a kind of "metalanguage" to serve as bridge between the other languages he used in this work: German, English, Czech, and Hebrew. This is the first English translation of the book, and the principal challenge in translating *Language and Reality* was to transform English into this "metalanguage," while nevertheless retaining Portuguese as a *basso continuo*.

The principal focus of Flusser's books and courses throughout this period was clearly the philosophy of language, but there is also acute evidence of technology as an emergent theme, especially the new science of cybernetics. Another important theme during this time period and that is clearly demonstrated in *Language and Reality* is translation as a theory of knowledge. For Flusser, translation as a theory of knowledge would subsequently develop into a working method for his unique style of thinking by way of using self-translation and taking on the task of translating his own texts into a variety of different languages as a way to refine and develop his ideas. After 1967, Flusser gradually ended the period of his work devoted to the philosophy of language and soon embarked on a new phase that would focus on his own type of communication theory, for which he is best known in media studies today. Between 1968 and 1971, he taught at the Armando Alvares Penteado Foundation, where he was one of the founding members of the foundation's department of arts and communication until he moved back to Europe in 1972, eventually to settle in France, where he would live until his death in 1991.

All of Flusser's books, courses, and essays of this early period work like an interlocking constellation, and the Flusser Archive Collection, created for Univocal, was edited with this structure in mind so that an international audience could gain access for the first time to Flusser's early production. In every book of this phase, the author touches upon the philosophy of language from a slightly different angle. Today, the idea of the symbiotic relation between language and reality is once again a topic of research; therefore this publication of Flusser's *Language and Reality* in English comes at an opportune moment.

Rodrigo Maltez Novaes
São Paulo, Brazil
August 2017

Introduction

One of the fundamental anxieties of the human spirit in its attempt to comprehend, govern, and modify the world is the need to discover order. A chaotic world would be incomprehensible, therefore meaningless, and to attempt to govern and modify it would be pointless. Human existence would be nothing more than one of the component elements of this chaos—a futile existence. Therefore a chaotic world, although conceivable, would be unbearable. The spirit, in its *Will to Power*, refuses to accept this. The spirit searches in the depths of chaotic appearances for a structure, thanks to which such chaotically *complicated* appearances may be *explicated*. This structure must work in two ways: it must allow for the placement of each appearance within a general scheme—it must serve, therefore, as a reference system; and it must allow for the coordination of appearances—it must serve as a system of rules. The structure must be both static and dynamic. By fixing an appearance's place through the static structure, we make this appearance apprehensible. By linking an appearance to another so that one becomes the consequence of the other through the dynamic structure, we make this appearance comprehensible. The first effort, the fixing one, is equivalent to a cataloging of the world. The second effort, the coordinating one, is equivalent to a hierarchization of the world. If successful, the first effort will result in a catalog of all appearances clearly defined, one after the other, and the second effort will result in a hierarchy of classes of appearances, perfectly deductible from each other. The world will be transformed from chaos into cosmos. We will then be able to say that the world, which is *apparently* chaotic, is *really* orderly. Or that there is an *apparent,* chaotic world and a *real,* orderly one. Considering that this structure of *reality,* or rather, this structure that is *reality,* is not yet discovered, and that our catalogs and our classifications are still imperfect, we can, with a certain amount of optimism, say that the spirit advances from *appearance* toward *reality.*

This optimistic assertion is in accordance with the legacy inherited by the Greeks. It was they who taught us that we can see through appearances (phenomena) what transpires in them *(tà onta)*. What transpires (the *onta*) are comprehensible (they are *noumena*). The discovery of *noumena* within the phenomena is equivalent to unraveling the truth (*aletheia,* the "discovered"). Philosophy, religion, science, and art are the methods by which the spirit tries to penetrate into reality through appearances and discover the truth. The effort, therefore, covers the entire territory of human civilization. Civilizations not dependent on the Greeks are engaged in the same effort, though they formulate it differently.

Despite its antiquity, and despite its vastness, the effort is, however, subject to serious objections, and these objections accompany, as a secondary theme, the symphony of human civilization. They are of a different order, but we can roughly distinguish three types of objections: those that deny the ability of the spirit to penetrate appearances (skepticism), those that deny *reality* (nihilism), and those that affirm the impossibility of articulating and communicating this penetration (mysticism). The first type can be called *epistemological objections,* the second *ontological objections,* and the third *religious objections.* Although coming from different directions, each one of these types of objection endangers the building of civilization and threatens to plunge us into chaos. As chaos is unbearable, these objections are practically unacceptable. Epistemological skepticism, ontological nihilism, and religious mysticism are impracticable teachings. They are refuted, practically, by the continuation of life, that is, by our experience of knowledge, reality, and the communicable revelation of truth. These are positions that can be assumed, for a short time, at fleeting moments, by isolated spirits. However, this refutation does not diminish the theoretical vitality of the objections raised. The mere possibility of these objections plunges the whole effort of the spirit, therefore all civilization, into a climate of superficial pragmatism, into a climate of frustration and inauthenticity.

There is no escape from this climate. There is, however, the possibility of confronting it, of acclimatizing, of living in it. This possibility lies in making the quest for structure conscious. If we know what we seek when we seek *knowledge, reality, truth,* and if we know it as clearly as possible, then the articulated objections of skeptics and nihilists, and the mute objection of mysticism, will lose their terror and will become bearable. We will find that *knowledge, reality,* and *truth,* which these objections claim to deny, are not what we seek. We will find that the structure we seek to discover, though less majestic and more modest than it at first might have seemed to us, remains untouched and untouchable by the objections raised. We may, despite them, continue to seek, that is, to live. Knowledge, though less absolute, will remain knowledge; reality, though less fundamental, will continue to be reality; and the truth, though less immediate, will remain true. We will even discover that absolute knowledge, fundamental reality, and immediate truth are nothing more than hollow concepts, but also unnecessary for the construction of a cosmos, and that in this sense, the objections can be accepted. In this somewhat restricted sense of the cosmos, our endeavor to comprehend, govern, and modify it will continue to be valid, and our life within it will not have been futile.

The objective of this work is to contribute to the attempt to make the structure of this restricted cosmos conscious. This book will propose that this structure be identified with language; that knowledge, reality, and truth are aspects of language; that science and philosophy are language research; and that religion and art are language-creating disciplines. Nothing in this aforementioned statement should be considered as original or shocking, or as a farce. The ancient wisdoms of our ancestors affirm it. *Logos,* the word, is the foundation of the world of the prephilosophical Greeks. *Nama-rupa,* the word form, is the foundation of the world of pre-Vedic Hindus. *Hachaim hakadosh,* the holy name, is the God of the Jews. And the gospel begins with the phrase *In the beginning was the Word.* Despite these testimonies, and despite the identification of the Christ with the Word, the affirmation of the identification of the structure of the cosmos with language continues to shock the modern ear. Today's philosophy forms the last link in the chain that has alienated us from language and from the closeness with which our ancestors lived with their language. The attitude of our philosophy in the face of language is twofold. We have the attitude of the logicians who see only its formal aspect and, from this restricted angle, affirm its tautology. For the logicians, identifying language with the structure of the cosmos would do nothing but affirm a skepticism, nihilism, and collapse into a kind of mute mysticism. And we have the attitude of thinkers like Heidegger, who, while feeling the ontological value of language, used it for a kind of word game. In this way, they violate language, forcing it to adapt to them rather than adapting to it. Nevertheless, both attitudes represent, in a certain way, the timid first step of current thought in its return to language. Pure mathematicians and *concrete* poets—the former use language in the sense of logico-mathematical philosophy, and the latter use it in the sense of Heidegger's philosophy—are almost consciously making contact with two of the roots of language. And both do it in their search for knowledge, reality, and truth.

In my identification of language with the structure of the cosmos, I intend that the concept of *language* encompasses both pure mathematics and poetry and that it surpasses both. In my attempt to define this concept—in fact an attempt frustrated by the very ontologically primordial position I attach to this concept—the advanced sciences that deal with language will be of little help. For them, language is one of the phenomena that constitute the components of what they call *reality*. If it were not so, there could be no language sciences. Science, as has already been said, is the attempt to catalog and classify appearances, and to each page of the catalog and to each class of appearances corresponds a specialized science. Language, taken as appearance, forms the field of one or more specialized sciences. But it is evident that language, considered thus as appearance, does not serve as the basis of the concept understood in this context. On the other hand, it will be impossible to completely ignore this aspect of language. The concept *language,* as it will be used in this work, will therefore include the aspects clarified by the specialized sciences.

I believe that I am exempt from proving that the ancient sages, when they spoke of *logos, nama-rupa,* or *hashem,* did not refer to the mathematical, poetic, philological, and etymological aspects of language. In this work, however, it is necessary to include the aspect of language meant by the sages, which could be described as *magical* or *holy.* It is well to remember, on this occasion, that the so-called primitive peoples, those who are therefore closer to the origin (if primitive and original are related concepts), endow language a supreme power. The mere knowledge of the name of an enemy confers power over it, and magic phrases can even force higher entities to serve the will of the initiate. This magical aspect of language, which is not the same as that of the ancient Greeks, Hindus, and Jews, should also be included in the concept of language as applied here.

Finally, it will be necessary to consider language as it unfolds within our minds, forming and governing all our thoughts. Suspicion will arise, and more than mere suspicion, of the identification of language with thought. The aforementioned aspects of language, however, will, I hope, prevent us from falling into that pure and simple idealism that an identification of language with thought could easily bring with it.

As you can see, the concept of language used here will be vast. However, it will contain nothing artificial or forced. On the contrary, forced and artificial are the narrower concepts of language. It is precisely these narrow concepts, to which science and philosophy have accustomed us, that bar our view of language in all its plenitude. The first effort of this work must therefore be to regain a naivety in the face of language, a naivety lost in the course of the history of thought. At first glance, this effort is doomed to fail, because naivety cannot be won. There is, however, the possibility of putting in parentheses the knowledge accumulated in the course of history, leaving it in suspense, as if available for future reference, and of approaching language without such knowledge, a possibility that requires violent mental discipline. Husserl called this discipline *phenomenology*. In this way, according to Husserl, we will achieve a second-degree naivety that will enable us to grasp the core, the *eidos*, of language. I doubt that we can keep up this violence against our mind for a long time. However, the phenomenological method will be the unreachable ideal I shall attempt to reach.

Thus will emerge, so I hope, albeit in a vague and hazy way, what I call language. If my statement has any grounding, the identification of this something with the structure of the cosmos should become evident to the reader. However, even if I can present the evidence, I will not have produced something that could be called a *philosophy of language*. I will have at most suggested some of the innumerable possibilities of establishing such a philosophy. And this is the intention of this work.

There it is: language, in all its immense wealth—the most

perfect instrument we have inherited from our parents and in whose development countless generations have collaborated since the origin of humanity, or perhaps even beyond that origin. It envelops within itself all the wisdom of the human race. It connects us to our neighbors and, through the ages, to our ancestors. It is at one and the same time the oldest and the latest work of art, a work of art majestically beautiful but always imperfect. And each one of us can work upon this opus, contributing, albeit modestly, to perfecting its beauty. Inwardly we feel that we are possessed by it, that it is not we who formulate it but that language is the one that formulates us. We are like small gates through which it passes and then continues on its way into the unknown. But at the moment of its passage through our little gate, we feel we can use it. We can regroup the elements of language; we can formulate and articulate thoughts. Thanks to our work, language will continue to be enriched in its advancement. By now, in this introduction, I venture to suggest that this is our role in the structure of the cosmos. But, on second thought, in formulating and articulating, are we not being humans in the most worthy sense of this word? Are we not, by this activity, fulfilling, and perhaps overcoming, the human condition?

1

LANGUAGE IS
REALITY

Our era is characterized by the mania of statistics. Tables, curves, and accounts invade the scientific and para-scientific literature as proof that we are a generation of accountants committed to compiling an inventory of the world: *data* are being compiled and compared in order to be computed. We are a generation of accountants who are in the process of becoming a line of computers. The goal appears to be an electronic superbrain that devours *data* and excretes statistics. However, there is a basic statistic missing: what elements make up the total sum of *data*?

The senses are instant data donors. Locke teaches us that *nothing is in the intellect that had not previously been in the senses*. The intellect being still an essential link between data and the electronic brain, the senses continue to be providers of data. The missing statistic must therefore clarify the extent to which the different senses participate in the supply of data. What percentage of data do we owe, for example, to touch or smell? How do you modify this percentage in the course of history? Is it increasing or decreasing? And in the course of an individual life? Does the contribution of smell increase or decrease with advancing age? What is the social distribution of smell? Does it contribute more (absolutely and relatively) to the worker or the intellectual? And what is its distribution between the sexes? And among peoples? The problem is complicated by the following consideration: the senses, in addition to being data donors, are themselves data. We are, therefore, facing a series containing elements that, in turn, contain the series. This is a problem of formal logic to be solved, in the future, by the electronic brain, because it apparently surpasses the capacity of the human brain.

In the absence of this basic statistic, I propose the following hypothesis: we are indebted to the ear and the eye for the large majority of data available to us, since the vast majority of such data consists of words heard or read. The great majority of what forms and informs our intellect, the vast majority of information at our disposal, consists of words. What we count with, what we compile and compare, and what we compute, in short, the raw material of our thinking, consists, for the most part, of words.

In addition to words, the senses provide other data. These are distinguished from words qualitatively. They are unarticulated, that is, immediate, data. To be computed, they must be articulated, that is, transformed into words. There is, therefore, apparently an instance between sense and intellect that transforms data into words. The intellect sensu stricto is a weave that uses words like threads. The sensu lato intellect has an anteroom in which a spinning wheel works that turns raw cotton (sense data) into threads (words). Most of the raw material, however, already comes in the form of yarns.

If we define *reality* as *data set,* we can say that we live in a double reality: in the reality of words and in the reality of *raw* or *immediate* data. As the *raw* data reach the intellect itself in the form of words, we can also say that reality consists of words and words in statu nascendi. With this statement, we have assumed an ontological position. The present work is an attempt to verify to what extent this position can be maintained.

1.1. Language Perceived from Without

The words that come to us through the senses come organized. They are grouped in obedience to preestablished rules, forming phrases. When we perceive words, we perceive an orderly reality, a cosmos. The set of perceived and perceptible phrases we call *language*. Language is the set of all perceived and perceptible words when they are linked together according to preestablished rules. Individual words or words stacked without rules, *babbling* and *word salad,* form the edge, the margin, of language. They are the chaotic extremes of the language cosmos. The study of language as it is perceived is equivalent to the research of a cosmos. Given our definition of reality as a set of words and words in statu nascendi, the study of language is possibly the only legitimate type of research of the only type of conceivable cosmos.

Words are the elements of the language cosmos. They correspond to atoms within the Democritean cosmos or to monads within the Leibnizian cosmos. They are perceived as clusters of sounds (when heard) or forms (when read). They are therefore divisible, just like the atoms of physics. Besides being perceived, words are apprehended. As such, they are indivisible.

Words are apprehended and comprehended as symbols, that is, as having meaning. They substitute something, they point to something, they search for something. What do they replace, what do they point to, what do they seek? The naive answer would be, *ultimately, reality*. The more sophisticated answer, from the existentialists and logicians, would probably be, *nothing*. The answer in this work will be, *since they point to something, replace something, and seek something beyond language, it is not possible to speak of this something*. Nevertheless, the fact persists: words are apprehended and comprehended as symbols, and consequently, the cosmos of language is symbolic and meaningful.

Symbols are the results of an agreement between several contractors. The early Christians agreed on the meaning of the sign of the fish: it will be the symbol of the Christ. The traffic service and the drivers have agreed (more or less precariously) on the meaning of a given sign: it will be the symbol of the prohibition of parking. From now on, the sign in question can be apprehended and comprehended by the initiate. What was the agreement, or agreements, that preceded and resulted in the system of symbols that is language? This question is still more naive than the eighteenth-century opinion of the social contract as the basis of human society. The origins of language and its symbolic character are lost in the mists of an impenetrable past. This is apparently a typical pseudo-problem: an agreement on the meaning of language presupposes its existence as the vehicle for such agreement. We are forced to accept language and its symbolic character as the very condition of thought, and the phrase *origin of language* therefore lacks meaning in this context.

Classically, different types of words are distinguished in view of their meanings. There are nouns that mean *substances,* there are adjectives that mean *qualities,* there are prepositions and conjunctions that mean *relationships between substances,* and there are verbs that mean *processes modifying substances.* However, it is evident that this classical division is absurd and cannot be maintained. It presupposes the existence of an absolute reality whose structure is being mirrored by the structure of language, approximating Plato, for whom the phenomenal world mirrors the structure of the world of ideas. Languages such as Chinese, whose structure makes it impossible to distinguish between nouns, verbs, and so on, prove that this presupposition is unsustainable. Either Chinese (and with it all syllabic and agglutinative languages) is *wrong* or the classical division is wrong. But in the field of the Portuguese language, the classical division does not work. In the phrase *Isto é uma caixa grande* (This is a big box), *box* would mean "substance," and *big*, "quality." In the phrase *Isto é um caixão* (This is a coffin), the quality would be swallowed up by the substance in a sort of metaphysical miracle that would outweigh all the deeds of the prophets. Not to mention the substantiation of adjectives and verbs, or the adjectivation of nouns and verbs, and so on, which are commonplace things within the Portuguese language but which are inconceivable juggling acts within the *absolute reality* presupposed by the classical division. It is therefore necessary to abandon this type of misapplied Platonism. We are, after all, too skeptical to be able to accept, unwittingly, a reality of *substances, qualities, relationships, processes,* and so on, just so we can classify words.

However, something of the classical division of words must be saved. Even if wrong, it is not entirely gratuitous and arbitrary. Nouns, adjectives, and so on, really exist in the Portuguese language. We must therefore say the following: language, as a system of symbols pointing to something, meaning something, looking for something, does not consist of equivalent symbols but of symbols hierarchically differentiated. The meaning of each symbol becomes understandable only within the whole system. In the case of the Portuguese language (which is a subsystem within the general system of language), and in the case of more or less related languages, this hierarchy takes the form of nouns, adjectives, and so on. But the hierarchical position of each word is fluid and is modified according to the requirements of the rules that organize the system.

Words come organized in phrases. The classical division, always subject to an extreme Platonism, and knowing exclusively fusional languages, distinguishes in the sentence the subject, of which the process treats and what the phrase means; the predicate, that is, the process itself; the object, the goal of the process; the attribute, which qualifies the subject or object; and the adverb, which qualifies the process, and so on. The basic idea of this division is this: absolute reality consists of substances that change, transferring qualities from one to another. These transfers are the situations of reality. The phrase mirrors, in its structure, this reality, if true, and fails to mirror this reality, if false. This classic division must be rejected for the same reasons as those discussed during the discussion of word classification. Far from being an analysis of the phrase, it is the result of the uncontrolled domain of the Portuguese phrase (and related languages) on the mind of the supposed analyzer. With the abandonment of the classical division of the phrase, we have also abandoned the classical concept of truth and the correspondence between phrases and reality. We must therefore arrive at a new concept of truth in the course of this work.

The fact that the classical division cannot be maintained is illustrated by the existence, for example, of agglutinative languages. These languages form sentences by putting words together, so that they lose their individuality and merge into a whole. To want to distinguish in them subject, predicate, and so on, would be to falsify their meaning. Either the phrases of these languages are neither true nor false, no more than mere noises, or the classical analysis of the phrase is wrong. It is, however, extremely painful to abandon the prejudices of the classical analysis of the phrase. Abandoning this analysis, we will be rationally restricting the territory of logic. Logical analysis and classical sentence analysis are, fundamentally, the same thing. Saying, as we are, that classical analysis is not applicable to languages other than fusional ones, and that, even in the case of fusional languages, it is applied with reservations, we are denying the universal validity of logic. Far from being a discipline of the human spirit, it appears as a discipline of the spirit governed by fusional languages, and more especially by Indo-European languages of the Kentum branch. If we consider that logic is the basis of mathematics and science, for which we claim universal validity, we will understand how difficult it is to abandon the classical analysis of the phrase. It is true that our mathematics and our science will still remain valid; however, they will be valid in a narrow epistemological sense. They will no longer affirm anything in relation to *reality-in-itself,* only in relation to realities such as the one of the Portuguese language.

However, we are forced to take this bold step. It compels us toward an analysis of the radically new phrase. According to it, the phrase is an organization of words, and this phrase is correct when it obeys the rules of the language to which words belong and incorrect when it does not obey them. When this organization of words takes place within my intellect, it is called *thought. Phrase* is the name of the objective aspect, and *thought* is the name of the subjective aspect of this organization of words. There are correct phrases and thoughts (when they obey the rules of their language), and there are incorrect phrases and thoughts (when they do not obey them). In the case of the Portuguese language and certain other languages, such as Chinese and Inuit, the rules are entirely different. In the case of Portuguese, we are in fact able to distinguish the subject from the predicate, from the object, and so on, not because an absolute reality requires it but because the rules of logic command it. But we cannot always make this distinction, or only very artificially at times, as these examples illustrate: *Chove* (It rains) or *Há gente em casa* (There are people at home). These examples, despite not being logically analyzable, are not without meaning.

There are, therefore, correct and incorrect phrases and thoughts. But what about true phrases and thoughts? This problem involves the relationship between phrases. Language has rules governing relations between phrases. A phrase (or a thought) is true, in relation to another phrase, when it obeys those rules and false when it does not obey them. In the case of Portuguese and related languages, these rules are logical and are called *syllogisms.* In other languages, the rules are different. Relative truth is, therefore, a purely formal and linguistic quality of phrases—a result of the rules of language. And what of the absolute truth, that classic truth of the correspondence between phrases and *reality*? The one I check when I say *it rains* and I look out the window? The correspondence between my phrase *it rains* and the raw data *it rains,* which I perceive through the window, is difficult to analyze. (This will be attempted, outlined, in the next section.) However, I can already say that I comprehend the data *it rains* only in the form of the phrase *it rains* and that, therefore, the famous correspondence between sentences and reality is no more than a correspondence between two identical sentences. The absolute truth, if it exists, is not articulable, so it is not comprehensible.

In summary, the raw material of the intellect, *reality,* therefore, consists of words and *raw data* to be transformed into words to be apprehended and comprehended. Words are symbols meaning something inarticulable, possibly *nothing.* The set of words forms the cosmos of language. That cosmos is governed by rules that vary from language to language. It is futile, to go beyond the limit of language, to speak about the origin of language and therefore about the origin of the meaning of the words and about the origin of the rules. Language, with its meaning and its rules, is the datum par excellence. The words observe a hierarchical order, which varies from language to language. Phrases, or thoughts, are organizations of words obeying rules that, in the case of Portuguese, are approximately logical. Truth is a correspondence between phrases or thoughts, a result of the rules of language. Absolute truth, this correspondence between language and the *something* it means, is as inarticulable as that *something.*

1.2. Language Perceived from Within

The intellect, with its infrastructure; the senses and their superstructure; and the spirit (or any other word) form the Self. The Self is therefore a tree whose roots (the senses) are anchored on the ground of reality, whose trunk (the intellect) carries the sap harvested by the roots (transformed) to the canopy (the spirit) to produce leaves, flowers, and fruits. Just as the tree consists entirely of modified sap (and, from the point of view of the sap, a channel through which the sap evaporates from the ground into the cloud), the Self is entirely made of reality harvested by the senses; it is a channel through which reality spills out into the future. But we know that the tree is more than just the sap.

Reality, within which the roots of the Self (the senses) suck avidly, becomes words upon reaching the trunk (the intellect). In this transformation, in this abrupt and primordial leap, in this *Ursprung,* lies the miracle and the secret of the origin of the Self. For the intellect, there is an insurmountable chasm between *raw data* and *word.* The intellect can plunge inwardly into its own depths in the urge to reach the roots; however, where the word ends (or begins), the intellect stops. It knows the senses and raw data they collect, but it knows them in the form of words. When the intellect reaches out to seize them, they turn into words. This is precisely the intellect: it consists of words, apprehends words, comprehends words, modifies words, reorganizes words, and transmits them to the spirit, which possibly overcomes them. The intellect, therefore, is the product and producer of language: *it thinks.*

However, in a curious way, the intellect feels the difference between word and raw data. When the senses send it ready-made words—that is, when I hear or read words—the reaction of the intellect differs from its reaction to raw data. In the face of raw data, unattainable, but intimately close, the intellect rushes upon a word, it articulates. In the face of the word, it comprehends and establishes immediate contact, it converses. Since the intellect consists only of words, and knows nothing but words, how can it distinguish, at the entrance door, raw data from ready-made words? The distinction is made on the basis of an aesthetic criterion: raw data come in the form of a chaotic folder; words come organized into phrases. The raw data come, for example, in the form of the following words: *it hurts, hard, brown, four legs,* which are equal to

I hit the table. Ready-made words, arriving already organized, are proof, and the only intellectually acceptable proof, of the existence of other intellects. If the senses did not provide the intellect with words organized in phrases, it would be doomed to solipsistic chaos. What turns chaos into cosmos is the possibility of conversation, the comings and goings of language.

If the senses did not provide the intellect with words organized in phrases, the intellect itself would not exist. The intellect is formed by learning words. The newborn child is, from the linguistic point of view, a *geometrical* place, where the intellect, that knot of words, can be realized. The newborn child is an organization of senses and an apparatus intended to maintain the senses. This organization is thrown into a chaos of raw, meaningless data. The senses siphon the raw data and react to them physiologically. The current of raw data entering the senses carries with it words spoken by the mother, by the *human* environment, that is, the linguistic environment, which surrounds the newborn child as a protective cover against chaos. To these words, the child reacts not only physiologically but also intellectually; it apprehends them. To apprehend words is to form intellect. The apprehended words begin to form a superstructure on the senses; a Self begins to appear in the strict sense. The apprehended words have meaning. Over the chaos of raw data without meaning, within which the senses live, the symbolic cosmos of words emerges, within which the intellect lives.

As the words seized increase in number, that is, as the intellect grows, the game of the rules governing the organization of words begins to function. The words seized begin to be comprehended. The activity of the intellect begins; intelligence begins. From the passive *entertained* (intellect), the active *to entertain* (intelligence) emerges. From now on, two processes develop within the intellect. It continually receives information from the senses: words and raw data. The words it apprehends. The raw data it translates into words, to apprehend them. And the apprehended words are regrouped; they are comprehended. The intellect thinks.

To these two processes a third one is soon added. Organized words, phrases, thoughts, begin to be expelled (German: *ausge-druckt*), expressed by the intellect in the direction of the senses. These are phrases; thoughts tend to *phenomenalize themselves*. The primordial ontological leap from raw data to word repeats itself in the opposite direction, and the intellect articulates. Henceforth it participates in the conversation of which Heidegger says *we are*.

A word of caution: everything that has been said in this section refers to that ontologically problematic region that sits between sense and intellect. It is therefore not really attainable by the intellect and cannot be authentically formulated into words. It should therefore be read, not as a report, but as an allegory. This is a desperate attempt, but no less necessary, by the intellect to comprehend itself. Allegory (the substitutive reading) is the only method available to the intellect in its attempt to overcome itself. But allegory is always equivocal, never univocal as the ideal symbol. To reduce the risk of equivocation, I shall resort to the testimony of some philosophers who, with their thoughts, penetrated this confused region.

What I have called *raw data chaos,* which tends to turn into words, does not, ontologically speaking, have the dignity of *Being;* it has the dignity of *becoming.* This is Schopenhauer's *world as Will,* which tends to become *world as representation.* This is Nietzsche's *Will* that tends toward *Power.* This is Bergson's *élan vital,* which tends to intellectualize itself. This is Heidegger's *Vorhandensein* (at hand), which tends to be recalled and transformed *(überholt)* by existence *(Dasein).* Each of these thinkers interprets differently this intellectually insurmountable but effectively transposed by a leap chasm between *becoming* and *Being.* When the intellect goes to this region, it thinks of what Nietzsche calls *den schwersten Gedanken* (the most difficult [or heavy] thought). This thought is a weight that the intellect cannot bear. The intellect is attempting to shift what

Hartmann calls *layer*; it is trying to shift its weight—an impossible task. However, all these resources of the mentioned thinkers are biased, a priori, by their unconscious captivity within language. Their philosophies are unconscious analyses of language. This renders their attempts doubly desperate. It renders *hard thinking* even harder than necessary.

I resume the thread of the argument. The intellect realizes itself through conversation. It becomes real in the sense of participating in the fabric of conversation, which is the horizontal cut in the current of language. If we consider language (as we are now obliged to do) as a set of words—that is, as realized raw data, such as the cosmos of *Being* emerging from the chaos of *becoming*—and if we consider that these words appear within us, as *intellects,* and in threads between these nodes, as *conversation,* we are then obliged to say that an intellect is realized in conversation. Language as a whole is the sum of the conversations and of the intellects in conversation through the ages. The intellect in conversations enriches language in two senses: it propagates itself toward the future, and it extends itself horizontally, increasing the number of words and combinations of words. It creates words and creates thoughts (phrases). The intellect in conversation preserves and increases the territory of reality. It realizes by realizing itself.

This is the ontological meaning of the expression *man as zoon politikon.* Society is real as conversation, and man is real as an intellect participating in that conversation. In this sense, we can say that society is the basis of reality and that man is real only as a member of society. However, in this perspective, language reveals itself as the essence, not the instrument, of society.

However, the activity of the intellect is not limited to the apprehension, comprehension, reformulation, and creation of words and phrases (thoughts) or to the articulation of these phrases (thoughts). The intellect bears upon its shoulders, like Atlas, a world of silence, into which thoughts (phrases) pour and within which they evaporate. To speak of this superstructure of the intellect is even more difficult than to speak of its infrastructure. All words seeking to mean it are flawed, because they are intellectual. This world of *spirit, intuition, immediate vision,* forms the canopy of the tree of the Self. Nothing else can be said about it, except that it is the sense, that is, the direction in which the thoughts of the intellect run and which represents an upper limit of language. Being supralinguistic, this world is supra-real, and in this sense, unreal, from the point of view of the intellect. It goes beyond the scope of this work and must be considered in this context only as endowing sense, that is, direction, to the processes of language. Language appears, from this angle, as a process seeking to overcome itself.

1.3. The Multiplicity of Languages

Suppose, for a moment, that there is only one language. In this case, the considerations set forth in sections 1.1 and 1.2 would not have occurred. The ontological problem of language would be masked to the point of never being discovered by the intellect. The epistemological problem of language would not exist. In this case, the problem of an extralinguistic reality could not have been discovered, and there would be no problem of knowing reality. There would be a perfect and unambiguous match between raw data and words. The word and raw datum would form a single set, the raw datum being the external aspect and the word the internal aspect of that set. The single language would be the inner aspect of reality, and reality would be the external aspect of the single language. The rules of the single language would be the internal aspect of the laws that govern reality, and these scientific laws would be the external aspect of the grammatical laws governing the single language. The distinction between *natural sciences (Naturwissenschaften)* and *sciences of the spirit (Geisteswissenschaften)* would be a distinction between two directions of research of the same set: the natural sciences would move from the inside out, the sciences of the spirit from the outside in. The single language would be identical to the human spirit, or at least to what Kant calls *pure reason*. In fact, if there were only one language, we would all be, of course, Kantians (that is, if that single language were German or a related language). The rules of the single language would be the *categories of pure reason* and would represent the internal aspect, the aspect of *knowledge,* of the laws of nature, which would be the *categories of reality.* The analysis of the single language would be the true *critique of pure reason.* The problem in which Kantian epistemology culminates—*are there synthetic a priori judgments?*— would acquire, in this hypothetical situation, its full meaning: *are there combinations of words that obey the rules of the single language and at the same time mirror relations between raw data? Therefore, is there knowledge?* The answer, in this hypothetical situation, would undoubtedly be affirmative. Unfortunately, this hypothetical and paradisiacal situation of the single language is not the case. The preestablished harmony (in Leibniz's sense) between language and reality is not the case. Pure reason is not identical to language *tout court* but to *one or more languages.* As a result, the *categories of knowledge,* the *categories of pure reason,* far from having universal and human validity, are contradictory and alternately applicable. I will give, for the time being, a single example. I will have the opportunity later to expand the theme: Kant distinguishes three categories of quantity, namely, unity (measure), multiplicity (size), and totality (whole). However, when pure reason thinks in Czech, it categorically distinguishes the following quantities: unity, duality, multiplicity up to four (organized multiplicity), multiplicity of more than four (amorphous multiplicity), totality in the plural, and totality in the singular. Kant's categories, far from being *categories of knowledge per se,* are, in essence, the categories of the German language.

The multiplicity of languages reveals the relativity of the *categories of knowledge.* Therefore the ontological and epistemological problem of language becomes evident. There are as many categorical systems, and therefore as many kinds of knowledge, as existing languages and potential ones. The tenuous relation between reason and *the thing in itself,* which Kantian philosophy establishes, is therefore at best a cluster of arbitrarily interchangeable yarns. The image offered is this: reality, this raw data set, is there, given and brutal, close to the intellect, but unattainable. It, the intellect, has a collection of eyeglasses, for the different languages, to observe the data. Every time I change my eyeglasses, reality *seems to be* different. The difficulty of this image resides in the expression *seems to be.* In order *to be,* reality must seem. So, every time the intellect changes its language, the reality is different. But an ontology that operates with an infinity of substitutable reality systems is intolerable. It is preferable to abandon the concept of reality as a set of raw data. It is preferable to say, as I did in the previous sections, that raw data are only realized when articulated in words. Thus they are not reality but potentiality. Consequently, reality will be the set of languages. This definition of reality circumvents the second difficulty implied in the image outlined herein. What is this intellect that changes eyeglasses? What is its reality? Within the new definition, the difficulty disappears: the intellect is not real unless it thinks in some language. The nefarious duality between *reason* and *the thing in itself,* between *matter* and *idea,* between all those poles of reality enshrined in the philosophical tradition, disappears with the identification of *reality* with *language.* All thinkers have always felt that this is a false duality, a pseudo-problem. The idealisms and materialisms of all ages testify to it. Viewed through the prism of language, the dichotomy disappears. The rectified image is now as follows: the intellect can become realized, and raw data can also become realized in various forms, that is, as different languages. Each language by itself is the place where raw data and intellects are realized. Or, describing the same situation differently, every language has two horizons, namely, the raw data that tend to realize themselves in it and the intellects that think about them. However, *raw data* and *intellect* are not real, they are not realized, except within a given language.

The problem of the natural sciences, this method of the intellect to study *reality* (raw data) seemingly without recourse to any specific language, emerges insistently and is no longer suppressible. The results of scientific research are apparently valid in all languages. However, rather than weakening the argument developed here, an observation of these results actually supports it. Science, sensu stricto, as we have known it in the West since the Renaissance, is equivalent, from this point of view, to the emergence of a new language. In it, raw data are realized in mathematical symbols. The intellects think of it with mathematical symbols. Being a recent language, it illustrates admirably how language in general works. The symbol *m* means mass, the symbol *sec* means the metric second; the symbol *gen* means the bearer of heredity, without regard to the *reality* of these meanings. Because science is a recent language, its independence from *the thing in itself* becomes more evident than in the case of ancient languages. This is the reason for the sense of unreality that pervades us when we enter the territory of the exact sciences. The explanation for this sensation is this: science, far from being valid for all languages, is itself a language to be translated to the other languages in order to be realized in them. But being a recent language, it is still incomplete. The intellect is able, in theory and practice, to think continuously in Portuguese or English. But the intellect cannot think continuously *in terms of science*; it cannot always think scientifically, and as a result, it must continually translate from *scientific* to Portuguese. Having to continually abandon the territory of the language of science, having to continually make the effort of translation, the intellect perceives more clearly the distance between word and raw data and is overwhelmed by the sensation of unreality. The translation and the sense of unreality that accompany it will, however, be the subject of the following section.

But some will say that science works independently of any translation. Airplanes fly, turntables play, and bombs explode, killing everyone, including those who cannot speak in scientific terms. This formidable argument of common sense against the thesis presented here can be applied to all languages, not just to science. The German who learned to make shoes in German can perfectly sell them to someone from China who speaks Chinese and who has never learned to speak German. The German language, like the scientific one, works independently of translation. At least so it seems at first glance. Under analysis, the argument becomes circular and therefore loses its validity. The bomb that kills me, the shoe that I buy, are raw data for me that I apprehend and comprehend in the form of Portuguese words. For the scientist and the shoemaker, they are also raw data, realized in the form of scientific symbols and German words. It is true that the position of the scientist and the shoemaker in the face of the bomb and the shoes is different from mine. The scientist and the shoemaker are the producers (in Greek, *poiités*) of the words *this bomb* and *this shoe,* and in this sense, they are also the artifices of the raw data that these words mean. However, the meaning of these words will remain inaccessible to me until I apprehend the *scientific* or German languages. For me, there are raw data only in relation to the meaning of my words. However, thanks to conversation and the possibility of translation, I can also apprehend the scientific and German meaning of the bomb and the shoe. Later I can identify my *bomb* with the scientist's bomb and then, in a sort of naive metaphysics, that it is the *same* raw datum. Strictly speaking, the argument must be formulated in the following manner: within the system of my language, science works independently of any translation. As it turns out, this is an innocuous argument. However, throughout the course of the discussion, problems of production and poetry arose. For systematic reasons, I must postpone this subject until the third chapter of this work.

Recapitulating and summarizing the order of ideas of this section, the multiplicity of languages illustrates and illuminates the position assumed in the previous sections and makes it more consistent. This multiplicity makes it evident that it is idle to speak of *extralinguistic reality* and demonstrates the relativity of *knowledge,* which is by definition limited to the field of a single language, because knowledge is a function of the categories of that language. During the discussion, science was revealed as one of the languages, and scientific knowledge was valid, that is, meaningful, only in relation to that language.

1.4. On Translation

Every language is therefore a complete system, a cosmos. It is not, however, a closed system. There are possibilities of connecting several languages; there are possibilities of moving from one cosmos to another. There is the possibility of translation. And there are polyglot intellects. We are, in the face of these two possibilities, again tempted to resort to a deaf and mute metaphysics. The possibility of translation seems to say that a phrase in the original form and in translation means the *same thing* and therefore *the thing in itself.* The possibility of polyglotism seems to say, *I can think in two different languages, so I am independent of the language in which I think.* The monster of *the thing in itself* and of the absolute Self raises its double head. It is necessary, in order to face this monster, to analyze with patience the seemingly simple process that results in the translation of a Portuguese phrase, for example, into an English one. The process has two distinct aspects. There is a connection between two sentences, one English and one Portuguese. And the intellect transports itself, translates, jumps *(übersetzt)* from the Portuguese cosmos into the English cosmos. Although they are two aspects of the same process, it will be good to distinguish them: one that seems to refer to *the thing in itself* and another to the absolute Self.

Let us take as an example the translation of the Portuguese phrase *vou* by *I go*. What allows me to say that one sentence is a translation of the other? The classic answer would be that there is a set called *the Portuguese language,* another called *the English language,* and a third set called *the reality of raw data.* The first two sets consist of symbols signifying the data of the third set. Each raw datum corresponds to a Portuguese word and an English word. The raw datum *vou* corresponds to the Portuguese word *vou* and to the English words *I go.* Therefore the translation is legitimate. As we have abandoned, at a considerable cost, the concept of a *raw data reality,* the classical answer does not satisfy us. We must reformulate it and say the following: there is a set called *Portuguese language* and another called *English language.* Both consist of hierarchically organized words and are governed by rules of word combinations. The hierarchies and rules of the two sets are similar. The hierarchical place of the phrase *vou* and the rules that stipulate its form are similar to the hierarchical place of the phrase *I go* and the rules that also stipulate its form. The role, that is, the meaning of the phrase *vou* within the Portuguese system, is therefore similar to the role, to the meaning, of the phrase *I go* within the English system. The translation is therefore approximately legitimate.

Our answer is more laborious, but it has the advantage of being more correct. It is easy to demonstrate that the classical answer is false. Just expand the sentence. *Vou estudar* cannot be translated to *I go to learn.* The meaning of *vou* is therefore not identical to the meaning of *I go.* In Portuguese, *vou* is an auxiliary verb, whereas the English *I go* is not, or, if it is, it is in a much weaker degree. The translation of *vou* into English is strictly impossible. There is no place within the hierarchy and within the rules of the English system that corresponds to the Portuguese *vou.* The English *reality* does not include *vou.* Given, however, the similarity, the kinship, between the two languages, I can translate, approximately, as proposed. The raw datum that *vou* and *I go* presupposedly mean has proved a myth.

However, we shall see that the difficulty of translation increases when wanting to translate the phrase *vou* into a language that is a little less similar, for example, into Czech. Several equally legitimate alternatives are offered: *jdu, chodím, chodívám,* even *Půjdu* can be chosen. All these phrases correspond to the Portuguese *vou,* but, within the Czech system, each has a place, a different meaning. The translation, and therefore the conversation, becomes dubious. The Czech reality distinguishes (1) *I will go now* = *jdu,* (2) *I usually go* = *chodím,* (3) *I rarely go* = *chodívám,* and *I go* in the future tense of *going* = *Půjdu,* and so on. Note that the translations offered here are also very approximate. The Czech and Portuguese realities are too different to permit a satisfactory translation of the phrase *vou.* The myth of the raw data has evaporated.

Another quick example of a language even more distant: wanting to translate *vou* into Hebrew, I will have to resort to *ani holech.* Formally, the Hebrew phrase says *I walker of the male gender.* This example, in itself, illustrates the profound divergence between the Portuguese and Hebrew ontologies, the latter of which has no verbs in the present. For Hebrew, an activity in the present has no meaning. I do not have to resort to more distant languages to illustrate what has already been demonstrated: the legitimacy of translation is a function of the kinship between languages. It is important, however, to note what kind of kinship is involved: not an etymological kinship, but an ontological kinship. Although the two are usually linked, this is not always the case. There is, for example, a curious ontological kinship between classical Greek and modern German, inexplicable etymologically but perceptible especially in philosophical speculation.

Before drawing a conclusion from this order of ideas, I want to consider the second aspect of translation, the apparent passage of the intellect from one language to another. In other words, what happens to me when I move from *vou* to *I go?* While I think *vou,* I am firmly anchored within the Portuguese reality. *Vou,* which is my thought, has a definite meaning. However, during the translation, during this ontologically inconceivable moment of the suspension of thought, I hovered over the abyss of nothingness. *I am* during this transition only in the sense of becoming. Under the prism of translation, the Cartesian cogito ergo sum acquires an immediate existential meaning. Up to now, existential thinkers seem not to have realized that nothingness, that horizon of Being, manifests itself as *nullifying* during the process of all translation. Any translation is annihilation. The existentially important fact in this process is the circumstance that this annihilation can be *überholt,* surpassed and overcome by the realized translation. Is this not, by any chance, a miniature version of death and resurrection? It is hoped that a phenomenological analysis of translation and a deeper study by existential thinkers might better illuminate this problem in the near future.

The leap from language to language, crossing the abyss of nothingness, creates in the intellect that sense of unreality so closely related to the existential anguish that was mentioned in the previous section, when science was discussed. The possibility of translation represents, for the intellect, the experience of the relativity of reality. *Vou* is situated within one reality, *I go* within another, and between both lies the abyss of nothingness and of the annihilation of thought. By translating, the intellect goes beyond the horizon of language, annihilating itself in this process. Without recourse to any mystical or religious view, the intellect *lives (erlebt)* the dissolution of reality and of the Self. The instinctive refusal of the monoglot (if you allow me to use such a word) to accept as equivalent the meaning of another language is a sign of a healthy repulsion against the ontological relativism that polyglotism brings with it. Whoever does not speak *one's own language,* or speaks more than one language, is suspect. This person has rightly lost the firm grounding of reality, which is precisely *one's own language.*

This consideration is mitigated by the unconscious concept we have of the mother tongue. Despite all the arguments to the contrary, we feel it to be the *true* reality. All languages are more or less successful attempts at an approximation of the reality contained in the mother tongue. And the Self not only thinks of it but loves it. This love is the last refuge in the face of the relativity of reality and explains, to a large extent, as I believe, the irrational power that nationalism exerts upon some human minds.

Translation provides us with the only truly practical distance from language. It grants us the possibility of comparing languages. It is mainly thanks to translation that the philological sciences work. Laws—like the laws of the natural sciences, governing the transformation of words, the transformation of rules, and the gradual passage from one stage to another of language until the formation of a new language—can be discovered. However, languages are not living beings. Drawing a parallel with biology is dangerous. Portuguese does not descend from Latin like the chick does from the chicken. Languages are open systems that permeate each other with great ease and promiscuity. Japanese is a good example. It is a mixture of so many incongruous languages that its classification within a *genealogical tree* becomes absurd. Greedy, every language absorbs elements of any other, assimilates and digests those it can, rejecting, as strange but integrated bodies, those elements that it is incapable of assimilating. The hierarchy of a language's words, and, to a lesser degree, the rules that govern it, is in continuous flux. The concept of *specific language* cannot therefore be well defined. In many cases, the transition from one language to another is gradual, between Portuguese and Spanish, and between Czech and Slovak. But the possibility of translation reveals that it is thanks to its ontological capacity, thanks to the reality that language provides to the intellect, that languages acquire their individuality. I want to close this section with an illustration of the unique personality implicit in all languages.

There are two types of translation: the meaningful and the lexical. The English phrase *I am afraid of the appointment I am going to have at the dentist tomorrow* will have the meaningful translation into German as follows: *ich fürchte mich vor der morgigen Untersuchung beim Zahnarzt*. The lexical translation would read, *dabin mit Furcht der Anfrage was ich gehe haben dem Zahner morgen*. The lexical translation from German to English would be, *I am afraid of the tomorrow research near the dentist*. The lexical retranslation of the phrase in English would be, *existence of the first singular person present along with fear belonging to the query what I am walking to do for the dentist tomorrow*. This kind of translation is grotesque. Why? Because it reveals the personality of one language in the clothing of another. The feeling of the grotesque, the impossible and the unreal, which we feel, to a lesser degree, when we hear a language spoken by those who do not master it, is proof of the ontological power and, finally, of the authenticity of every language. When we come to deal with artificial languages, this theme will be approached more closely.

Summing up, the possibility of translation is one of the few possibilities, perhaps the only practicable one, for the intellect to overcome the horizons of language. During this process, the intellect annihilates itself provisionally. It evaporates when leaving the territory of the original language so as to be condensed once again when it reaches the language of the translation. Each language has its own personality, providing the intellect with a specific climate of reality. Translation is therefore, strictly speaking, impossible. Translation is approximately possible, thanks to the similarities, ontological similarities, between languages. The possibility of translation decreases with the diminution of similarities. All of this complexity reveals, with an even greater force, what was settled in the previous section: the ontological relativity of each language.

1.5. Current Distribution of Languages

See *the attached language map* [appendix]. The number of possible
or imaginable languages is unlimited, however, the number of
languages available is small. By itself, this circumstance is not
surprising at all. Speaking *classically,* it is to be expected that few
language possibilities would have been realized, given the relative
youth of language (hence of humanity) in relation to the age of
mother Earth, for example. If we consider, however, the breadth of
the variations made, the doubts and the hopes for a link between
language and the reality of raw data emerge again. In fact, there are
basically only three types of languages: fusional, agglutinative, and
isolating.[1] There are, therefore, only three kinds of worlds within
which the human intellect lives.

The world of fusional languages consists of elements (words)
grouped into situations (phrases = thoughts). Within a situation,
an element retains its identity and enters into relationship with
other elements. There are rules governing the modifications of
the elements in different situations, and there are rules governing the structures of situations. The elements and rules vary from
language to language, but the basic character of this world is the
same: elements come into contact with each other, thus changing
but retaining their identity. The world is in flux; it is dynamic;
situations follow each other, but the elements, *substances, attributes, processes,* and so on, are relatively constant. Each situation
is constituted in such a way that we can distinguish in it a center
(the subject), a process that the center irradiates (the predicate),
and a horizon toward which the process is irradiated (the object).
There are situations of difficult analysis that seem to want to hide

---

1   At the time when the book was written, this was the current structure
    of language classification. Today, the field of linguistics has widened
    the classification spectrum. However, the structural differences that
    Flusser discusses are still valid and pertinent. [T.N.]

the subject, the object, or the predicate. They represent epistemo-logical and ontological problems, to be solved according to the rules of the respective language. These rules can be codified and expunged from contradictions. Thus coded, they will be valued as a prototype of the system of rules of any fusional language and will be called *logic*. No fusional language is logical in itself, but every fusional language is reducible to logic. In short, the world of fusional languages is a dynamic world, consisting of plastic but constant elements, obeying rules reducible to logic. This world is a chain of organized situations.

The world of agglutinative languages consists of superwords (thoughts). When the logical spirit, the one who leaves the field of fusional languages to investigate the territory of agglutinative languages, begins to analyze these superwords, it discovers that they represent a conglomeration of words and half-words (mistak-enly identified with the prefixes, suffixes, and infixes of fusional languages), which correspond, vaguely, to our phrases. The su-perword vaguely means *that* which is a situation in the world of fusional languages and which is signified by the phrase. But in the territory of the agglutinative languages, there is no situation of elements; there is only the nonanalyzable *hic et nunc*. As this meaning is impenetrable to our spirit, I will give an example, the Inuit superword *igdlorssuatsialiorfigssaliarqugamiuk*. In this superword, the analyzer discovers the following: *ig* = house, *dlor* = suffix, *ssu* = large, *a* = suffix, *tsia* = untranslatable, *fi* = place, *gss* = future, *a* = suffix, *lia* = to walk, *r* = suffix, *qu* = command to do, *gam* = when it is for him, *iuk* = end of the superword. The attempt to translate it into a fusional language results, as the author quoted above (Kaj Birket Smith) attests, in *it happened that he asked to go to the place of future construction of the relatively large house*. But the author arrived at the translation, as he confesses, not so much by the analysis of the superword as by the observation of the effect on the interlocutor. One more example, a simpler one, but a revealing one: the word *I* is translated to the Inuit by *uvanga*. Analyzing this little superword, we find *uva* = here and *nga* = suffix, meaning vaguely *as for me*. Under analysis, the Inuit word *I* reveals itself to be circular, containing itself. I believe, in view of the examples given, that the world of agglutinative languages is impenetrable for us. The most we can say is that it is a compact world, consisting of blocks of meaning. For us, this is a chaotic and meaningless world.

The world of isolating languages consists of a few elements (syllables) with no specific meaning, which are used as stones of a mosaic to form sets of meaning (thoughts). For example, the syllable *qi* in Cantonese can acquire the following meanings, among many others, in certain groups: *history, to employ, corpse, market, army, lion, to trust, to serve someone, poetry, time, to know, to gift, to be solid, to lose, to proclaim, to look, ten, to raise, stone, generation, to eat, house, clan, beginning, to release, to experiment, business, power, official, to swear, to die, to happen,* and so on. The set formed by the syllables, therefore, that which corresponds vaguely to our phrases, emanates an aura of meaning, certainly univocal with Cantonese, but equivocal in our eyes. For example, the same set can also be translated into Portuguese as meaning *few see much of anything strange* and as meaning *the more a man has seen, the less he wonders.* The sets are formed, apparently, without any rule. The syllables are not modified and are not linked together, remaining isolated within the set. Every combination of syllables produces meaning. The set forms an aesthetic whole, whose experience *(aistheton)* is the aura of meaning. This aura, since it is not logically univocal, cannot be grasped in the fusional languages. The world of isolating languages is therefore impenetrable for us, and the most we can say is this: it consists of a few harsh and immutable elements, which, having no meaning, are not as much a part of as they are the condition of that world. (As, for example, atoms are not parts of matter but the condition of the formed molecules.) These elements form aesthetic sets, without formal rules (except, perhaps, for aesthetic rules), which emanate an aura of meaning. If the ideal of the fusional phrase is truth, then the ideal of the syllabic set is beauty. Of course, we will be falsifying this problem when formulating it in Portuguese and therefore in a fusional language.

These are, roughly speaking, the three types of languages that exist. As stated in the previous section, it is not possible to define exactly one individual language. Every language is an open system, accepting elements from outside, including languages of a different type. The syllable *dao,* for example, entered our languages, retaining within them some of its original ambiguity, meaning for us something between *path, center,* and *god.* On the other hand, the character of every language is a problem in itself and cannot be strictly classified. Fusional languages, such as German and Sanskrit, present agglutinative tendencies, which bear witness in words like *Donaudampfschifffahrtsgesellschaft* and *satchitananda.* The first means *Danube society of steam navigation* and the second *being-knowing-happiness = enlightenment.* A fusional language like English evidences isolating tendencies, which can be witnessed in words like *get* and *put* that acquire their meaning only within a sentence. Nevertheless, in general, we can say the following: fusional languages prevail in the European and Indian peninsulas of the Eurasian continent and in the territories between the two peninsulas, except Turkey. Isolating languages prevail in the southeast and east of the same continent. Agglutinative languages prevail in the north and northeast of the same continent. The other continents and archipelagos are dominated by groups of languages that tend to the agglutinative or fusional type (which, for not having, however, produced *civilizations* in the sense of resulting in *philosophical systems,* will be omitted from this work). This is fertile ground whose ontological exploration will certainly bring interesting results in the future.

Fusional languages have Western civilization as a consequence, including the Islamic and Indian ones. Isolating languages resulted in the Eastern civilization, including the Japanese one, whose language, despite being basically agglutinative, was saturated with Chinese elements to the point of losing its personality. In the course of history, agglutinative languages formed the background of the two civilizations, a background that periodically threatened to engulf both civilizations in chaos. The approximate current situation is illustrated in the attached map [appendix]. In it are seen the three main trunks in their approximate geographical distributions. Seen horizontally, the map represents the current state of language distribution. Viewed vertically, it represents, very schematically, a theory of the history of languages. To preserve relative clarity, many languages were sacrificed, and the modern branch of the Indo-European languages was omitted.

There are, therefore, three, and only three, types of languages within the infinity of possible languages. The human intellect is realized only in three different ways. Raw data are apprehended and comprehended only in three basic forms. And although it is not possible to translate authentically from one form to another, conversation between them is not at all impossible. There are transpositions and attempts at translations that capture a residue of their original meanings, though certainly distorted and corrupted. There is, therefore, an almost inarticulate foundation common to all three systems. This common ground is the spectrum of the hypothetical single language from which all languages would have emerged. According to this idea, we should imagine a paradisiacal stage of language, *before the construction of the tower of Babel,* during which the situation outlined in section 1.3 would have prevailed. However, I do not think we need to resort to this kind of false historicism to explain the tenuous link between different types of languages. We know nothing, and will never know, of this original hypothetical language not only because we lack the means of investigation but mainly because it would be something inhuman and therefore incomprehensible. This single original language would, as discussed earlier, be identical with absolute knowledge and should be abandoned together with the concept of paradise. We are forced to accept, without the possibility of explanation, the multiplicity of languages in their three types and the precarious possibility of communication between them. To want to overcome the limits of this multiplicity that is imposed upon us would be to want to go beyond the limits of language. This attempt, like any attempt to overcome language, condemns us to silence.

The human intellect is realized in three ways, and two of them, the fusional and the isolating, have created this curious kind of conversation called *civilization*. Two creative conversations are developing on the globe, and every attempt at authentic communication between them is so deeply misleading as to be virtually impossible. *Oh, East is East and West is West, and never the twain shall meet.*[2] The peaceful and violent incursions of one into the other will be judged in their ontological aspect in the third chapter of this work.

I summarize what was discussed in this section as follows: within the infinity of possible languages, only three types were realized—the fusional, the agglutinative, and the isolating. The fusional is the world of logically organized situations. The agglutinative is the world of solid and amorphous blocks, of *hic et nunc*. The isolating is the world of mosaics, of aesthetic ensembles. The fusional world gave rise to the conversation called *Western civilization,* and the isolating world gave rise to the conversation called *Eastern civilization*. They are two distinct realities with different values. The agglutinative world is, from the point of view of these civilizations, the chaos of babbling; it is barbaric, in the Greek sense of that word.

---

2 Rudyard Kipling, *The Ballad of East and West.*

1.6. Universal Languages

The great conversation that is Western civilization has, therefore, an implicit ontology as origin, provided by the structure common to all the fusional languages. It has a prejudice toward reality, to which none of us can escape. Theoretically, it is possible to turn against this ontology, to want to get rid of this prejudice. The history of philosophy proves it. However, because all our thoughts are organized according to the rules of fusional languages, and run the risk of becoming meaningless and turning into word salads, all our arguments against our basic ontology already assume it to be valid. The structure of reality is, therefore, categorically imposed by a fusional language upon our intellect. The problems of Western thought are fundamentally formal problems of language. Western philosophy can therefore be regarded as a more or less unconscious search for the structure of fusional languages. Science can be seen as an attempt to rediscover the structure of fusional languages in *nature*. It cannot therefore surprise us that Eastern philosophy (if we understand anything about it) seems to have nothing in common with ours but seems to be a completely different discipline. Much less does it surprise us that science in the Western sense of the word, that is, the chain of observation, induction, deduction, and generalization, can only emerge and exist in the West. The cultural colonization that the West is currently pursuing, transplanting its philosophy and science into nonfusional territories, will certainly yield unexpected results. Philosophy and science characterize Western civilization better than any of its products. Although unconsciously, these disciplines expose the structure of language: philosophy unveils the internal aspect of language, science its external aspect. Both do so by the same method: abstraction. The structure of fusional languages is inviting toward abstractions; it causes them. The situations that make up our world are not unique and incomparable, as the agglutinative blocks and isolating sets must be. They are comparable in structure. The situation *Joseph has an apple* and the situation *John loves Mary* are comparable by their structure. It is therefore possible to abstract from the concrete situation its concrete aspect and to stick with what is common to the two comparable situations. What remains is the structure of the situation in the form *ArB*. This arbitrarily composed formula would be a phrase of an abstract language—a language that would have universal validity for every fusional language that knows concrete situations like *Joseph has an apple*. Philosophy and science are attempts to establish such abstract artificial languages. If these attempts are successful, the Western conversation will be greatly facilitated, because all Western languages would be translatable into such new language.

However, the task is a lot more difficult than it seems. Fusional languages, although having the same type of structure, do not have identical structures. The situation *Joseph has an apple* does not have the same structure in Russian, where it takes the form *Near Joseph apple*. The formula *ArB* does not apply to the Russian situation, because Joseph is no longer subject, that is, the center of the situation, but the indirect object. The situations *Joseph has an apple* and *John loves Mary* are not directly comparable in Russian. As a result, the attempts of philosophy and science should be made to become ever more abstract so as to encompass the maximum of concrete structures. But in this process, they always become less meaningful. Formal philosophies, such as logical symbolism, have a much more universal validity than existential philosophies or so-called *life* philosophies. Existential and *life* philosophies are practically valid only to the languages in which they are formulated, as I shall endeavor to demonstrate later. Logical symbolism probably applies to all fusional languages; however, it gained this vastness for the price of the loss of meaning. Exactly the same statement can be made regarding science. The more exact, that is, abstract, it becomes, the greater its field of validity and the smaller its meaning becomes. Physics, which can now formulate its sentences in very few mathematical symbols, probably represents the pinnacle of what is attainable in the attempt to formulate the implicit structure of fusional languages. In this rough sense, physics really *explains* reality. Yet its meaning has become so narrow that physics is dangerously approaching tautology. Wittgenstein's philosophy crossed the same path in the opposite direction and consciously achieved the same pinnacle of perfection. This universal artificial language valid throughout the West will, when achieved, be tautological and meaningless. A word of caution: in this section, I used the word *meaning* in the sense of this abstract artificial language signifying phrases from natural fusional languages, that is, concrete situations.

Philosophical speculation, together with its logical symbolism, scientific research, and mathematical symbolism, are not the only attempts to establish universal Western languages. They are, however, the only attempts with some probability of success. It should be noted, however, that the attempt can be made in the opposite direction. Instead of abstracting the concrete aspect of the situation, it is possible to condense this aspect and thus to formulate a Western universal language that would be opposed to the language of logical symbolism and mathematics. This would be an attempt to construct a language in such a concrete way that its structure, although always typically fusional, would be very simple. The world of such a language would represent the lowest common denominator to Western languages. It would be the reduction of the Western conversation to a common base of infantilism or cretinism. The hope would lie in the fact that perfect understanding is possible among Westerners in the lower tier. This attempt was made in the form of *Basic English*. A fusional natural language was chosen as the starting point, English. The structure was reduced to very simple situations, consisting of a few subjects and objects and very few relations between them. Seventy percent of Basic

English words are nouns, 18 percent are adjectives, and 2 percent are verbs. In total, the language consists of 850 words. We are, therefore, in a world consisting of approximately 600 substances with approximately 150 attributes that are related to each other in approximately 15 different ways. The 600 substances of this world are interchangeable; they are the objects and subjects of 150 properties in 15 different ways. What is significant, however, and proves the limitation of the possibilities of this attempt, is that 10 percent of Basic English words are *grammatical* words, therefore belonging to its pure structure. The attempt to infantilize and cretinize the Western conversation seems, therefore, doomed to failure. Only someone who speaks English can really grasp the meaning of the 10 percent of Basic English grammatical words. The aesthetic result of the attempt is noteworthy. It reveals the aesthetic quality of authentic languages, which I shall deal with in the third chapter of this work. I will give as an example, and without commentary, a phrase that is not exceptionally beautiful in the English original, simply because the difference between the original and the Basic English one will be further emphasized: a soup very common in England is made of oxtail and is called *oxtail soup*. In *Basic English*, it is rendered *water of end of male cow*.

Basic English is a philosophical and scientific attempt to build a universal language, albeit in the opposite direction. It is, therefore, most interesting to note that the same infantilization and cretinization of the fusional world occurred spontaneously, when it invaded the isolating world, China. I refer to *Pidgin English*. This is the spontaneous attempt of the isolating intellect to grasp the meaning of our world. There is a rather accidental resemblance between the two languages. Pidgin English consists of 65 percent nouns, 13 percent adjectives, and 10 percent verbs. The remaining 12 percent are words from native languages and are therefore impossible to classify logically. Pidgin English has approximately six hundred words. It can therefore be considered as a more successful attempt than the scientific Basic English. From China, it has spread through the Pacific and is spoken by several million people. To illustrate the result, I give as an example an excerpt from Psalm 23: *The Lord is my shepherd, I shall not want; He maketh me to lie down in green pastures; He leads me meekly to calm waters.* In Pidgin English: *Bigname watchen sheepysheep, watchum blackfella, no more belly cry fella hab. Bigname makum camp alonga grass; Takum blackfella long walkabout, no fightem no more hurry wata.* The reader who knows how to speak English may judge from this example how far Pidgin English can convey the meaning of the psalm to the mind of a Chinese person who has achieved the certainly very difficult task of learning that language.

The innumerable attempts at artificial universal languages, like Esperanto, Ido, and Volapuk, are halfway between logical symbolism and Basic English. By attempting a universal language through a simultaneous movement between two opposing directions, they appear to be doomed, ab initio, to failure. If we look for utilitarian purposes, such as commercial and social exchange, and not ontological purposes, such as an exchange of basic ideas, I believe that some authentic fusional languages can serve as better examples of an authentic universal language. For the educated strata of the Far West, Latin served as a lingua franca during the Middle Ages, Italian during the Renaissance, and French during (and to some extent more recently English) the Enlightenment. In this sense, the most perfectly realized example of an authentic universal language is Greek, which served as *koiné* for almost all social strata during the classical era. This *koiné* is the language of the New Testament, so it became a sacred language for a considerable part of the West.

The great conversation that is the Western civilization turns, in ever wider circles, around a few primordial situations. Dilthey calls them *Urworte* (original words). These are situations that reveal and conceal the ontological foundation of our world. They reveal it, because they are articulated. They conceal it, because the situations are condensed to the point of merging and confusing meaning into a compact situation of very difficult analysis. The more these situations are analyzed, the more aspects they reveal. Western civilization, from this point of view, is nothing but a progressive analysis of the primordial situations that have been imposed on us. All our religion and art, all our philosophy and science, and all the instruments and institutions deriving from them are the result of this analysis. Among these situations, three stand out. The first comes from the world of Semitic languages and is the Hebrew phrase *Jehovah ekhad* (God-name one). The second comes from the world of Satem languages and is the phrase in Sanskrit *tat tvam asi* (you are this). The third comes from the world of Kentum languages and is the Greek phrase *gnothi seauton* (know yourself). Needless to say, the three proposed translations are flawed. In light of the argument developed in this work, the first phrase means, when very superficially analyzed, the inarticulable and inaccessible foundation of language (of the *holy name*). The second phrase means the identification of the spirit with the world, which resides precisely in language—*you* as the inner aspect and *this* as the external aspect of language. Hindu sages affirm it almost expressly when they postulate *nama-rupa* (name-form) as the basis and origin of the world. The third phrase means the indication of the way, the direction, the method of all knowledge. Knowing oneself, that is, knowing within oneself the structure of language, one will discover the intellect, the concealed (*aletheia,* "truth"). The structure of language (*logos,* primitively perhaps, "phrase") is identical to the structure of the world. This order of ideas, implicit in the primordial phrase, becomes explicit in Heraclitus. *Logos,* and the logic emanating from it, is the very foundation of language and reality. *Logos* is god (in the form of Hermes and Orpheus in Orphism and in the form of Athena in Olympism), which makes the world meaningful. Later, more explicitly still, *Logos* is the God of the Stoa. *Logos* is, for Christians, the second person to God, the first being the *holy name* and the third *pneuma* (breath, speech). The New Testament states, *In the beginning was the Logos* [the Verb].

The three primordial situations are, therefore, supplementary. They affirm, in three different ways, the ontology imposed on us by the structure of fusional languages. They show the three paths open to language and its reality: faith, meditation, and logical research. The advance through these paths, initially separated, later intertwined, is the history of Western civilization.

The languages in which the three primordial phrases are formulated are considered *holy*. However, of course, this is a case of three distinct types of *holiness*. Hebrew is *holy* because it is the language of faith, the language in which the *holy name* speaks to us. Hebrew is the language of the conversation between humanity and what transcends it. Prayer has value to the Jew only when pronounced in Hebrew. For the Catholic and Orthodox Christian, the Greek, Latin, and Slavic languages replace Hebrew in direct substitution. The translations of Hebrew into these newer languages are considered to be *inspired*; they are second editions of Hebrew. For Protestants, the situation is a bit more complex. However, for them, their language also retains the character of holiness from Hebrew. Luther's German and the English of the King James Bible prove it. This quality of *holiness,* which emanates from Hebrew and which spills over successor languages, makes such languages the *universal* languages of faith. This is a type of universality totally different from that understood by science and philosophy or by artificial languages. It is the result of a magical quality. A special and extreme case of these faith language successors of Hebrew is Arabic. In Arabic, it is not only the structure of the phrase and the form of the word that emanate magic but also the very structure of the word. Each letter has its magical and invocative power, and the very form of the written letter, the arabesque, aids the conversation with the transcendent. The analysis and discussion of this magical, *holy* quality of language are reserved for the third chapter of this work.

Sanskrit is *holy* because it is the language of meditation, the language into which the intellect dissolves. As the yogi says, it is not possible to attain enlightenment and to break the shackles of illusion without uttering certain Sanskrit words, for example, *Om.* The word *brahman,* when pronounced with disciplined breathing, has this invocative power. In fact, the word *brahman,* as it is spoken, has a quality of roundness, of being whole and full of meaning that invokes the absolute *it. Self,* both in the relative sense of *intellect* and in the absolute sense of *living cosmos* (the last stage to be abandoned in the progress toward *brahman*), is a kind of breathing; it is *atman.* This mystical quality of Sanskrit is harder to grasp than the magical quality of Hebrew for the European intellect. But European mystics do not ignore it. Our word *amen,* descendant of *Om,* proves this. Pali, the successor language of Sanskrit, is the mystical vehicle of Buddhism. Zende, the twin language of Sanskrit, in which the *Avesta* were written, was the mystical vehicle of Zoroastrianism. The magical–mystical quality of Arabic certainly owes much to Páhlevi, successor of Zende and the language of Persia when occupied by the Mohammedans at the very beginning of their conquest of the world. This mystical aspect of the *holiness* of language will also be analyzed and discussed in the third chapter of this work.

The *holiness* of the Greek language is less mysterious. I use the word *holiness* in this context mainly to preserve a parallel. However, as I will try to prove, the term is not being abused. The Greek words have a very special, ontologically fundamental meaning in our philosophical speculations and are therefore irreplaceable by others. Among the many possible examples, I cite some: *idea* (image of being), *phainomenon* (what appears, transpires, and shines through), *aletheia* (the covert to be discovered), *hyle* (formless substance), *Logos* (word, phrase), *on, onta* (being, beings), *poïesis* (fabrication), *musiké* (that which is inspired by man from the mouth of the gods), *physis* (the living world), *theoria* (recreational trip). We all know that these examples, taken from the vastness of words of ontological meaning, are being translated into Portuguese very inadequately. The evocative quality of the reality they emanate in Greek is lost. All those who have ever been interested in philosophy know that Greek words are irreplaceable. During the Middle Ages, Latin replaced Greek. For example, *substantia* meant *hyle* and *natura* meant *physis*. We know that the result of this substitution was an impoverishment of philosophical thought. One dimension of this thought evaporated in translation. Indeed, much of the philosophical speculation of philosophers like Heidegger consists of phenomenological analyses of Greek words. They are looking for that quality of *holiness* that I have in mind. It will also be the subject of discussion and analysis in the third chapter of this work.

I will summarize the argument developed in this section as follows: conversation in the territory of fusional languages resulted in Western civilization. Despite having the same type of structure, these languages differ from one another. Each one has its own structure. Philosophy attempts to construct a universal language that is common to all, the language of symbolic logic. Wittgenstein and the logicians came closer to this language. However, it threatens to be tautological. Science, with its mathematical language, is the other aspect of the same attempt. Physics has moved further in this direction, threatening also to lose all meaning in the sense of being translatable into authentic languages. The other possibility for the construction of a universal language is the lowest common denominator between all the fusional languages. This possibility was carried out approximately by Basic English and resulted in infantilism and inauthentic cretinism, which is proved by its repulsive aesthetic quality. Yet there are authentic universal languages, albeit in a different sense. They are the *holy* languages. Hebrew and its descendants are the universal languages of faith. Sanskrit and its descendants are the universal languages of mysticism. Greek and, to a much lesser extent, Latin are the languages of logical poetry. Western conversation is unique in that it revolves around a few phrases of ontological significance imposed by the type of structure common to all fusional languages. The *holy* universal languages maintain and propagate Western conversation.

1.7. The Limits of Translation

The civilization of the Far East is the result of the conversation in the territory of isolating languages. This is a conversation in which we do not participate. It is, for us, raw data. As such, it is apprehended and comprehended by us in the form of words and phrases of fusional languages, and it is in this form that Eastern civilization participates in our conversation, the Western civilization. Eastern civilization therefore has for us a reality different from Western civilization. We have immediate access to Western civilization because that is what we are. Eastern civilization *in itself* is for us part of the raw data world; it is part of the *thing in itself* and is accessible only through our language. In this sense, Eastern civilization is part of Western civilization. A discussion of the East is therefore only legitimate in this sense. Nevertheless, this discussion can be fruitful, not so much for the understanding of the East but for the understanding of the West. I say this because it is possibly a gratuitous and meaningless comparison for the East.

In the course of the preceding section, it became more and more apparent that the history of Western civilization could be regarded as the search for a universal language. This search gives our civilization the character of dynamism and progressivity. Our civilization has an ideal, possibly unattainable, toward which it flows. Given the threefold quality of the *holiness* of universal languages, this ideal is triple sided: ethical in the case of the languages of faith, aesthetic in the case of mystic languages, logical in the case of speculative languages. In the East, this search for a universal language does not exist. The East has this language: the writing of ideograms. It lacks, therefore, the dynamic and progressive aspect of the West. The ideal toward which the West develops already lies in the source of the East. Eastern writing, the ideograms (a typically Western name), must therefore reveal something of the character and ideal of the East, at least for the Western spirit.

The Chinese characters used throughout the Far East and called *kanji* in Japan consist of brush strokes arranged strictly within rectangles. They give us an impression of strongly repressed chaos. They can be classified *roughly* into three groups: those that have a similarity, although very close, to objects, or pictograms; those that evoke, by association, a syllable of the spoken language, or phonograms (this happens, for example, if the same character is used to designate *fang*, "square," and *fang*, "aromatic"); and finally, those that resemble neither objects nor syllables, or ideograms. This classification, as well as being artificial, is flawed because large numbers of characters are represented by compositions of simpler characters of different types. Mandarin consists of approximately 420 syllables. The universal written language consists of hundreds of thousands of characters. This simple comparison suffices to show that the East does not think in syllables but in written characters. The attempt to classify the characters is therefore equivalent to the attempt to classify Portuguese words according to the images they evoke. In such a classification, the word *bico* (beak), for example, would be pictographic, because the *ic* suggests something pointed. And the slang word *bico,* meaning *temporary job,* would be phonographic. For not suggesting anything, the word *homem* (man) would be ideographic. It is better, therefore, to abandon all attempts at classification. Chinese characters are the raw material of the Eastern intellect; they are the way raw data are apprehended and comprehended. Illiteracy in China must have an epistemological aspect unknown in the West. In the East, spoken language must be a still imperfect first stage of written language.

Only the *literate* really has a developed intellect. The characters are apprehended in a somewhat parallel manner to the way we look at figurative paintings. The *message* and the aesthetic quality of the character are simultaneously apprehended and comprehended. The character that means *peace* not only does so because it consists of two characters meaning *roof* and *woman* but also for the aesthetic quality that it emanates. The same character can be written in several ways, highlighting this or that brushstroke. The *peaceful* meaning of the character changes accordingly. In the East, calligraphy has, therefore, an importance comparable both to our philosophy and our poetry. The calligrapher formulates his thoughts. The conjunction of two or more characters produces that aura of meaning discussed in section 1.5. For example, the character meaning *business,* followed by the character *old* and the character meaning *cause,* creates an aura of meaning that can be expressed in Portuguese approximately as *Why should we follow the ancestors?* Or *The old method does not apply to this business.* There are several styles of Chinese writing. These represent diverse mentalities to a much greater degree than art styles represent diverse mentalities in the West.

Let us now try to imagine the world in which the Easterner lives. He apprehends and comprehends raw data in the form of characters. For him, the world therefore has an aesthetic visual quality that escapes us. If a parallel is permissible, I will say that he thinks through abstract paintings. The *yin-yang* symbol, which we translate separately as *the female element* and *the male element* and jointly as *God* or *world,* represents the attempt to formulate an ideogram encompassing all ideograms. The ideograms *Dao* and *De,* to cite two more examples, and which form the basis of what is called *Daoism* in the West, represent, if contemplated, a whole range of experiences that together can be very vaguely called religious. It is interesting to observe what happened to Buddhism, that is, to a religion coming from a fusional field, when it entered the

East. The mystical meditation of the Indians turned into aesthetic contemplation and gave rise to Chan (in Japan, Zen) and therefore into something totally different. Western meditation, including Indian meditation, seeks a mystical union with *it,* the union between subject and object. Eastern contemplation seems to be the immediate experience of the inarticulable aesthetic whole, of the super-ideogram. The introduction of Buddhism to the East seems to have resulted in an *incorrect translation,* though an apparently very fruitful one. The introduction of our science will surely bring results as unexpected as those of Zen. The reception that Zen and other Eastern *philosophies* are currently having in the West—a reception certainly based on a series of bad translations, which must be evaluated together with other apparently *Orientalizing* phenomena, such as abstract painting and existential philosophy—could be considered an attempt, frustrated ab initio, to overcome the limits imposed on us by the structure of our languages. This theme will be discussed more fully in the third chapter.

However, it is art, and more especially Eastern painting, which seems to be able to communicate something to us from that world. The Eastern painter is a calligrapher who has overcome the limitations imposed by the ideogram. When we contemplate his works, something of the aesthetic quality of the abandoned ideogram penetrates our spirit. Yet this something is entirely inarticulable. When we try to articulate it, we are already falsifying it. In this contemplation resides, perhaps, the only possibility of an authentic communication with the East. The East is, however, passive and silent. To our intellect, the Eastern world of isolating languages is impenetrable.

The agglutinative languages did not result in civilizations in the sense we give to this word. The Mongols, the Tartars, the Turks, the Huns, all these ill-defined linguistic groups that erupted periodically into the territory of the two civilizations to sow terror and destruction, represent chaos for us. It is quite impossible for us to imagine how they thought. Their thoughts, these pieces of words and quasi-words glued to each other by debris of words, are meaningless to us. Gestalt psychology seeks to analyze the world of animals, the *unarticulated*. It tells us that the animal finds itself in a diffuse and amorphous world in which unregulated data appear that acquire an erratic meaning insofar as they affect the animal directly, thus entering the animal's *Gestalt* (things that are good to eat, things that serve for copulation, things that are dangerous, etc.). In contrast, the world of men is organized and has a meaning in itself.

I am afraid that *Gestalt* theory is unconsciously influenced by the structure of fusional languages and that psychologists confuse the structure of these languages with the *Gestalt* of the world. However, if we are to give credence to this psychology, then those who speak agglutinative languages live in the amorphous and diffuse world of animals. This conclusion is, of course, absurd. The existence of agglutinative languages alone proves that the world is being apprehended and comprehended through them, that there is a *Gestalt*, although imperceptible to our intellect. The superwords, which for us are blocks of *hic et nunc*, frustrated attempts at articulation, are meaningful to those who understand them. They reveal to them the structure and meaning of *reality*. This is, however, a reality that is forbidden to us. For us, this reality is veiled in a more radical way than the reality of the world of isolating languages. Although we do not understand the Eastern reality, we are in sympathy with it. Our categories of thinking cease to function in it, but their effects can be incorporated into our reality. The reality of agglutinative languages simply does not exist for us. The world of agglutinative languages is given to us raw, not as meaning something, as the world of isolating languages is, but as something to be signified. All we can say about this world comes from outside and has no function in this work.

The argument of this section is summarized as follows: the two language trunks in which we do not participate produce realities inaccessible for us. We realize, however, that the reality of isolating languages is composed not so much of spoken as of written elements. The ideogram is the element of thought in the field of isolating languages. The apparent conversation between this field and us, between syntactic words and isolated drawings, is, therefore, basically impossible. There is, however, a possible sympathy between the two worlds, a sympathy that can be experienced during the contemplation of works of art. The world of agglutinative languages is, for us, chaotic, diffuse, and amorphous. There is no possibility of spiritual contact with such a world. It has therefore been established that our research into language and reality must necessarily be restricted to the field of fusional languages. This restriction will thus be consciously applied during the course of this work.

Conclusion

The ontological position that this work proposes to investigate is that the *reality* of raw data is apprehended and comprehended by us in the form of language. This position is radical, because if it is accepted, the reality *as such* of raw data becomes inaccessible and, in this sense, empty. In section 1.1, the idleness of wanting to speak of this reality *as such* was clarified. Language must be accepted as raw data par excellence, and its rules must be accepted as the structure of reality. Knowledge is the result of observing these rules. Absolute truth, that is, the correspondence between language and reality *as such,* is as inarticulable as that reality is *as such.* In section 1.2, the problem was discussed from the point of view of the knower rather than from the point of view of the known. The *Self* was demonstrated as being a product and a producer of language, realized by language and realizing itself in conversation. The inarticulate regions of the Self, both the vegetative one of the senses and the intuitive one of the spirit, were, however, left open as being beyond the scope of this work. In section 1.3, the multiplicity of languages, and therefore the relativity of the realities of language, was discussed. It was illustrated how each language represents an entire cosmos. Knowledge is valid, strictly speaking, only in the field of a single language. In section 1.4, the possible connection between the different languages was investigated. Translation was interpreted as the destruction and rebirth of the intellect. Polyglotism appeared as a kind of multiple life of the intellect. Translation and polyglotism were recognized as the only intellectual methods for overcoming the limits of language. In section 1.5, verified was the existence of three types of languages, representing three types of reality. In section 1.6, the reality of languages of the fusional type, to which we belong, was discussed and the attempts to artificially articulate this reality were presented. Authentic articulation by the *holy* languages was also considered. In section 1.7, the attempt was made to discuss the reality of the other types of languages, an attempt recognized as impossible.

The investigation of language, or rather of languages, corresponds, according to the argument developed here, to the investigation of reality, or rather, of realities. It is certainly not the only type of investigation of reality possible. However, it is the most immediate. It is, necessarily, restricted to the field of fusional languages. Philosophical and scientific inquiry is ultimately nothing more than a more or less unconscious investigation of the structure of fusional languages. This is what I propose to analyze in the next chapter.

2

Language Shapes Reality

Wittgenstein is the thinker who has most deeply penetrated the problem of language. He defines philosophy as a set of bruises that the intellect accumulated by colliding against the borders of language. However, Wittgenstein always speaks *about language,* as if there were only one, never considering the plurality of languages. As a result, language is at the same time underestimated and excessively valued. What he knows *of language,* he also knows *of philosophy.* Even a superficial analysis of the thoughts of the various philosophers reveals, however, that these thoughts are the results of the language in which they are being formulated. Philosophical thoughts are, like any thought, phrases of a given language. They are meaningful and can be understood only within the set of that language. They refer to the reality implicit in that language. If translated into another language, they acquire a new meaning, slightly or more than slightly different from the original meaning, but certainly not intended by the thinker. We must say, then, that there are as many philosophies as there are languages that contain philosophical thoughts. What we call *Western philosophy* is, in effect, a conversation between different philosophies, a conversation based on more or less flawed translations. A self-conscious philosophy should be a research of this conversation and should aim to make these translation failures evident. In this way, philosophy would be a conversation that has as its subject the conversation itself. The conversation would be what is conversed. It would be an authentically reflective discipline, but not necessarily tautological. This creative power curiously escaped from the Wittgensteinian observation—both the creative power of conversation in general and the creative power of reflexive conversation in particular. Hence Wittgenstein's unjustified pessimism. He did not notice that language is not static but is something that grows and expands—grows and expands thanks to the intellects participating in the conversation. Thinkers like Husserl and Heidegger come very close to this understanding of the problem but never penetrate it. Heideggerian philosophy is a quasi-conscious study of some aspects and some words of German and Greek, more especially of the word *Sein* (approximately, "Being"). Feeling, though, that the problem is basically linguistic, trying desperately to create new words like *Zuhandensein* and *Anwesen* (untranslatable) and translations for Greek words (ontic, ontological, etc.), Heidegger never gets a clear glimpse of the problem. Hence the inauthenticity of the words created by that prophet of authenticity. The reason for all this is that a conversation has never been established between Wittgenstein and Heidegger, between the left wing and the right wing of the philosophical army that attacks the borders of language.

This conversation needs to be established if we want to avoid what Heidegger calls *Gerede* (roughly "small talk") and that desperate silence in which Wittgenstein dives. It can be established with certain advantages on a neutral terrain like Portuguese, which serves as a reference system for translations and retranslations. It is necessary, however, always to keep in mind the distortion that the translation causes and to rectify this distortion as much as possible.

This is a formidable task that may be the work of the present generation and future generations. Once carried out, it will coincide with a reunification of the Western conversation sensu stricto, now divided into two main currents, which we can roughly characterize as the continental current and the Anglo-Saxon current. In a way, it will be the rebirth of what the Scholastics called *philosophia perennis*. For this to be achieved, a certain amount of preparatory work, while humble in nature, will become indispensable. Part of this initial work will be the investigation of the ontological structure of the languages in which the philosophical conversation develops. The discussion that will be the subject of this chapter is an attempt to introduce an investigation into this.

What is the *ontological structure* of language? That which makes phrases meaningful. I say *structure* because this is something formal, a system of reference, and I say *ontological* because the meaning of language is reality. Instead of saying *ontological structure,* I could have used the expression *system of categories.* I avoided this expression because it was used in the course of philosophical conversation with such different meanings that it became equivocal. Aristotle introduced the concept. The word *category* means roughly *expression, phrase.* Aristotle distinguishes ten categories: substance, quality, relation, action, passivity, state (habit), situation (position), quantity, place, and time. For Aristotle, these are the ten ways of Being. Why? The observation of the list and the translation of the word *category* reveal it: because they are the ten elements of the ontological structure of the Greek language. (Note that in the preceding list, the Aristotelian categories were translated and therefore distorted.) The Aristotelian categorical system is the result of the analysis of Greek grammar. Aristotle was almost aware of this, or he would not have used the term *category.* Through the course of the history of philosophy, however, this origin of the expression has fallen into oblivion. Philosophers define *categories* as the basic forms of Being and knowledge (categories of reality and categories of knowledge). The nefarious dichotomy between the known and the knowable has become institutionalized. The relation between the categories of reality and the categories of knowledge has become the theme of epistemology. In this, as in so many other philosophical problems, Aristotelian influence has become a heavy burden. A great many (and among them Nietzsche) have preferred, therefore, to abandon the *category* concert. Nowadays, however, the construction of categorical systems is once again becoming a favorite pastime for modern ontology. (E. V. Hartmann, *Kategorienlehre*, 1923; Nicolai Hartmann, *Der Aufbau der realen Welt*, 1940). Independently from the ontological structure of the Sanskrit and Palli languages, the Hindu philosophers constructed categorical systems (sankhya, vicharchika, nyaya), which in our eyes seem to be very complicated and grotesque. I prefer, in view of this, to abandon the expression *category* and forget the tradition that it carries with it.

Every fusional language has a different, but somewhat similar, ontological structure. This similarity allows for the comparison between structures. We can, for example, say that *time* is part of the structure of all fusional languages, in the same sense in which we can say that the *queen* is part of the game of chess. Time will be the first element of the structure, whose analysis will be slightly outlined in the following section. I will try to illustrate what function it has in four fusional languages: two Germanic languages (German and English), one Latin (Portuguese), and one Slavic and therefore a little more distant (Czech).

2.1. Time

I will start by comparing four sentences that have a meaning that we can call, vaguely, the future:

> a. German: *ich werde gehen*
> b. English: *I shall go*
> c. Portuguese: *irei*
> d. Czech: *Půjdu*

These sentences are equivalent; that is, they are translations of themselves. However, they do not have the same meaning; that is, they do not mean the *same thing*. The phrase *ich werde gehen* points to the future because it contains the verb *werden*. According to the structure of the German language, the verb *werden* when accompanied by an infinitive means *the future,* when accompanied by a past participle means *passivity* (*ich werde geschlagen* = I am being beaten, someone beats me), when accompanied by an adjective means *to become* (*ich werde rot* = I become red), and when by itself is practically untranslatable into Portuguese. Since, however, the Portuguese intellect wants, at all costs, to penetrate German thought, it creates the forced translation (*werden = devir,* "becoming"). Please note, however, an authentic translation: *Es werde Licht, und es ward Lickt* = May there be light, and there was light. These examples do not exhaust the role of the verb *werden* in the ontological structure of German but already illustrate something of the meaning of the future tense in German.

I will say that this future has a character of passivity, of spontaneity, and of inevitability. (*Ich werde gehen* = I am walking, I am being made to walk, I must walk). There is a force within the German reality that pervades, shapes, transforms, and propels it toward the future, and that force is called *werden*. All things, to be real, must be possessed by it, must *werden*. This force is eschatological. The phrase *es wird Fruehling werden* illustrates this aspect. The approximate translation is *the spring shall be realized*. It's the end of time. This future tense pervades the whole German language. Destiny in German is *Geschick* (the commanded, the commandment, the inevitable). Close relatives of this word are *geschehen* (to happen) and *Geschichte* (history). History is, therefore, a series of events inevitably linked. It's the *werden* process. The very future in German is *Zukunft* (the approaching). We are, therefore, passive in the face of the events that approach us, as commanded.

This concept of the future in German makes German philosophical thinking about history, and especially Hegel, understandable. The Hegelian philosophy of history with its dialectical processes is an unconscious analysis by the author of the word *werden*. Also his *Phänomenologie des Geistes* (approximately the phenomenology of the spirit) is an analysis of *werden,* from another point of view. In Nietzsche, through a careful examination, *werden* assumes the form of the will to power and of the eternal return of the same (compare this with Goethe: *das Werdende, ewig wirkt* = the self-evolving, eternally realizing). (Note also that return = *Wiederkunft* and future = *Zukunft*.) In Heidegger, *werden* takes the form of *Geworfensein des Daseins* = the thrownness of being here). And here, I'm only referencing, for the reader, three examples. A conversation with German philosophy presupposes an understanding of the word *werden,* a much deeper understanding than this light discussion can provide.

The phrase *I shall go* means the future because it contains the verb *shall*. According to the structure of the English language, the verb *shall,* when accompanied by the first person pronoun, means *the future*. When accompanied by nouns or pronouns of the second and third persons, it means *duty*. The verb *will,* when accompanied by nouns and pronouns of the second and third persons, means *the future*. When accompanied by a first person pronoun, it means *to want*. Both verbs are defective; they do not know the future. To translate, *deverei* and *quererei,* I will have to use other verbs. A dialectical process in the sense of the German *ich werde werden* = *I shall become* is therefore impossible, because it is inconceivable. The atmosphere of both verbs is ethical and therefore practical. *Shall* represents the obligatory side and *will* the voluntary side of the action. The future is, therefore, the ethical aspect of the present, the appreciation of the present. It is, therefore, the aspect of the present perceived by the future (Kant's *praktische Vernunft*). (Note, in passing, that *Vernunft*'s translation as *reason* is flawed,

although generalized. *Vernunft* comes from *vernehmen* = to perceive.) English distinguishes two practical, ethical aspects of the
present: the obligatory aspect, seen from the first person, and the
voluntary aspect, seen from the outside world.

The hybrid character of that language hampers the analysis of
the ontological structure of English. German and Latin elements
intersect in English. However, despite this, the active and practical character of time is clearly seen. Time is always conceived as
a work, in the practical and ethical sense of the word. The past
is conceived as a work done by me (I *have* gone, in the sense of
doing the walking and now it is mine), when viewed subjectively.
And the past is conceived as a work done to me (I *am* gone, in
the sense that the walk was done to me and now it is part of me)
when viewed objectively. History is a continuous work. *What works*
is, for that very reason, real. *What does not work* has no meaning.
The denial of reality is the denial of work (I *do* not go = I will not).
However, it should be noted that the operational aspect is valid only
for what is *temporal* (accidental) and not *essential*. The denial of *I
am* is not I *do* not am but I *am* not. The denial of *must* is not I *do*
not shall but I *must* not. The phenomenal (accidental) character of
time in English becomes evident as not being part of the essence
(substance) of things.

The combination of idealism and empiricism, so typical of
English philosophy, can be understood as an attempt to reconcile
the verbs *shall* and *will* on one side and the verb *do* on the other.
Shall and *will* mean the ethical aspect of the essence that causes
time, that of *do*. The philosophies of Locke, Berkeley, and Hume
are attempts to penetrate through *do* until reaching *shall* and *will*.
They are operative epistemologies in search of an active ethics.
Pragmatism and thinkers like Russell and Whitehead, with their
working, operative hypotheses and their concepts of truth as *what
works,* are other examples of *do* in pursuit of *shall* and *will*. The
apparent parallel between James and Nietzsche is misleading and

a good example of a conversation between the deaf, that is, a conversation based on a false translation. In Nietzsche, as in James, *the Will* is postulated as the basis of reality. In Nietzsche, as in James, truth is devalued and subjected to the Will. The *summum bonum* for both is the realization of the Will (*success* for James and *Macht = power* for Nietzsche). Hence the impression of the Germans that James is a superficial Nietzschean and the impression of the Anglo-Saxons that Nietzsche is a pragmatist. However, *vontade = Will* and *vontade = Wille* do not mean the same thing. In the first chapter, I drew the reader's attention to the fact that an etymological kinship does not necessarily imply an ontological kinship. *Wille* is one aspect of *werden*; it is the imperfect form of becoming. *Macht* is the other aspect of *werden,* the realized becoming. *Wille* does; *Macht* did. Therefore the correct translation of *Wille zur Macht* is not the traditional *Will to Power* but *everything can be, willing.* James's concepts operate in a completely different world. *Will* is the future imperative of the objective world. *Shall* is the obligatory, but not necessary, future of the human person. Truth and knowledge emerge when *shall* operates upon *will*; they are operational, instrumental concepts. The truth is, therefore, good. All of James's philosophy is bathed in ethics, while Nietzsche professes to have surpassed ethics; he is beyond good and evil. The consideration of these two philosophies thus contributed to clarify three points: (1) how the ontology of their respective languages is implicit in them, more especially the concept of time; (2) how philosophical conversation can progress only after clarifying the problems of translation; and (3) how a philosophy can enrich its language.

The phrase *irei* (I shall go) means the future because it contains the suffix *ei*. According to the structure of Portuguese, the future meaning arises when the infinitive of a verb has a suffix added corresponding to the verb *haver* (there being) conjugated in the present. The verb *haver* originally means something very close to *ter* (to have). There was, however, a subtle shift in the structure of the

Portuguese language, which is still under way. In the course of this transformation, the verb *ter* has usurped the place of *haver*. The two most important refuges of *haver* are presently the impersonal *há* (there is) and the formation of the future. Both are in grave danger. The impersonal *há* is threatened by *ter* and the formation of the future by the verb *ir* (to go): *farei* = I shall do. *Haver* will most likely be eventually deposed. In the case of the future, this will probably happen because the tendency of language is to substitute suffixes for auxiliary verbs. We are, therefore, in the case of Portuguese, facing a concept of the future in the process of transformation. Let us consider, first, the old form. The verb *haver,* which gives rise to the meaning of the future, suggests a property, a quality. If I have something in the form *hei* (I have to), that is, if that something is mine in the form *tenho* (I have), that something is my property and qualifies my position. The future, in this Portuguese form, is, therefore, a property, a quality of the present. If we consider that a form of the past in Portuguese is formed by the auxiliary verb *ter,* for example, *tenho ido* (I have gone), we must conclude that this accidental and qualitative concept of time pervades a whole side of the time category in the ontology of the Portuguese language. I refer in this context to the Aristotelian categories mentioned earlier in this chapter. Among them, time is one of the accidents. The Portuguese language agrees in this respect with Aristotle. The German and English languages disagree with him, because in them, the future, as illustrated, is not accidental but substantial. However, in Portuguese, time reveals itself to be a quality, a property of substance. Therefore, from the Aristotelian point of view, it is not an independent category but a subcategory, since the Aristotelian categorical system predicts the category of quality. The concept that governs my thinking when I say *irei* is not, therefore, categorical in the narrow sense. I am not really thinking of time. I am thinking of a property of mine, namely, what I have at my disposal. In this restricted sense, time is not a category of the

Portuguese language, as it is in the case of the English language. In Portuguese, I have a future, just like strength, health, or money. If I am not aware of this, if I do not realize this lack of the category *time* in Portuguese, this is due to the archaism of the verb *haver,* which hides the meaning *ter.* Only a phenomenological analysis as outlined here makes this meaning resurface.

However, this analysis would not be complete if we were not to consider another aspect of the verb *haver,* namely, the submeaning *dever* (duty). *Hei de ir* = I have to go. In this most curious form, which is difficult to analyze, *ir* appears as an amorphous substance of which I participate. Compare *Hei de ir* with *Tenho de ir tudo* (I have to go all out). A phenomenological analysis of this form should bring to light aspects of the Portuguese future that approach the English *shall,* however, without ever becoming confused with it. Compare, in this sense, *Hei de ir* with *I have to go.* Unfortunately, this chapter being only an introduction to the analysis of phenomena like this, a continuation of this argument becomes impossible.

The reason for the discontent of the Portuguese language with its concept of the future becomes more evident; in other words, the fundamental reason for the shift from *irei* to *vou ir* becomes more evident. The Portuguese language is creating the *time* category, and, for that, it is creating a new auxiliary verb, the verb *ir.* This authentic revolution in the ontological structure of Portuguese is a beautiful illustration of the creative power that language possesses. The verb *ir* means to change one's position and has something to do with space. If we turn our attention again to the Aristotelian categories, we find that two accidental categories seem to be encompassed by the meaning of the verb *ir*: position and space. This seems to me to be proof of how the ontology of the Greek language is inapplicable to modern Portuguese thought. The verb *ir* as auxiliary verb joins three Aristotelian categories, as seen in these examples: *vou devagar* (I go slowly) = position, *vou para casa* (I go home) = space, and *vou escrever* (I will write) = time. This is a new vision of reality that we can observe, in its mathematically formulated result, in today's physics. Compare the meaning of *ir* in Portuguese with Einstein's space-time and Heisenberg's indeterminacy principle. Portuguese and her sister languages, French and Spanish, are the field from which the revolution that is happening to the concept of time and space in modern physics emerged. An analysis of French philosophy would, I believe, reveal the influence of the *Je vais aller* on the mathematics and physics of today.

Turning now toward Czech, and therefore to a language of the other branch of Indo-Germanic languages, belonging to the Satem branch, we must note a brutal fact: the future in the sense in which we think of it, simply does not exist. There are, indeed, a large number of ways in which I can translate *I will go* into Czech, but these forms are not equivalent to each other. Since Czech has an exotic ontology for the reader unfamiliar with a Slavic language, I will limit my efforts to give you a taste of what in Czech corresponds vaguely to the role of the future tense in translation. A translation of *I will go* is *budu chodit,* which is approximately *I will be a continuous walking.* Example: *In April I will attend the school,* which would be in Czech *In April I will be a continuous walking inside the school.* This is the only form of the future grammatically conceivable in Czech. As it turns out, it is formed by the verb *to be* and has a very restricted meaning. Another example: *Today I will go to your house,* which would be in Czech *Today I-go-near next to you.* *Prijdu* = *I-go-near* is grammatically present and owes its vaguely future meaning to the prefix *pri* = near. The Czech language allows a very large series of prefixes that create an aura of future meaning, at the same time radically altering the meaning of the verb. In the present case, *prijdu* does not mean, properly, *I will go* but rather *I will arrive.* Other examples: *najdu* = *I-go-over* or *I will find,* *vyjdu* = *I-go-out* or *I will walk,* *dojdu* = *I-go-to* or *I will come,* and so on. How, then, could one translate the meaning of *I will go?* The

closest seems to be *Půjdu* = *I-go-after* or *I will follow.* This is how
the translation is usually done. But a word of caution: the reader
may conclude that the prefix *po* = *after* indicates the future. This is
not the case. In the case of *píšu* = *I write,* for example, the closest
translation of *I will write* will not be *popíšu* = *I-write-after* or *I will
describe* but *napíšu* = *I-write-over* or *I will end up writing.* As it turns
out, the prefixes change the meaning of the verb in a way that must
seem erratic in the eyes of a non-Slav. The affix *over* turns *I will
go* into *finding* and *to write* into *ending up writing.* The prefix *after*
turns *I will go* into *following* and *writing* into *describing.* Note also
that the use of prefixes leaves a large margin for individual fantasy.
I have ample freedom to create my own meanings, in the hope of
creating that meaning which is loosely grasped by my interlocutor
on the basis of the known meaning of the prefix and the verb. The
lability of the prefixes is one of the sources of wealth, beauty, and
flexibility in Slavic languages.

What can we conclude from this quick glimpse of the future in
Czech? The distinction between present and future is not clearly
established. Czech has an indubitable future, formed by the verb
to be, but that future encompasses only a small part of the Portuguese future; it is, so to speak, an extreme future. The rest of the
territory of the Portuguese future is roughly signified by forms of
the present with variable prefixes. The spirit of a Slav, when he or
she thinks in the future, slips imperceptibly and gradually from
the present to the future. Only the extreme future, that distant
budu psát = *I will be a continuous and uninterrupted writing,* is actually perceived as future by Slavic thought. *Tomorrow I will write a
letter* = *zítra napíšu dopis* is felt to be more present than future.
As a result, the concept of time in Czech is radically different
and hardly comparable with the concept in Portuguese. I hope I
have transmitted at least a vague idea of this concept, because its
formulation in Portuguese is impossible.

The Czech language is the only one among the four here compared to have an authentic future of the verb *to be. Serei, I shall be,* and *ich werde sein* are future composites and therefore retain, in their meanings, some flavor of the auxiliary verbs. *Budu* is a simple form, structurally comparable to the Portuguese form *vou.* The Czech language is therefore the only one among the four compared that conceives a future to be ontologically separated from the present. The future in Czech is a different and distinct form from the present; there is a present form of being and a future form of being. They are two distinct realities. The various composite forms, formed by the prefixes, are attempts by the language to overcome the ontological abyss that separates these realities. The present and the future are two extremes among which are processed the composite forms of verbs with dubious reality.

A phenomenological analysis of language should consider all forms of time in all languages and should consider the corresponding mechanism in those languages that have no forms of time. However, for the purpose of this work, the comparison of the four forms of future is sufficient. The four languages compared are similar. They belong to the Indo-European family of languages. Translations between them are done constantly. There is an intimate coexistence between them. However, the analysis undertaken in the previous pages reveals that what we call *time* is a consequence of language structure and that, because the four structures are slightly different, time is slightly different in the four languages considered. This difference can be practically neglected in many contexts, and it is this possibility that makes translations possible. However, this is a basic difference, and its contemplation helps one to understand how thought works. We can therefore conclude the following: the ontological structure of the four languages considered (and presumably of all the fusional languages) produces the meaning *time,* and this meaning varies from language to language, according to their respective structures. As we translate, we leap from meaning to meaning. Time is not, therefore, a *category of knowledge* or *a way of looking at things* (Kant's *Anschauungsformen*), or even less a category of *reality,* as traditional philosophies make us believe; rather, it is a variable grammatical form that informs our thoughts (phrases) according to the language in which we think at a given moment.

2.2. Activity and Passivity (Subjectivity and Objectivity)

Fusional languages are organized in phrases. Unless these are defective, as, for example, the phrase *chove* (it rains), we can distinguish in them, under logical analysis, a subject, an object, and a predicate. In the sentence *Eu escrevo um livro* (I write a book), *I* is the subject, *a book* is the object, and *write* is the predicate. The phrase can be reversed as follows: *Um livro está sendo escrito por mim* (A book is being written by me). The second form is the reflection of the first. It is as if they had put a mirror in front of it and we were reading it in that mirror. Now *a book* is the subject and *by me* is the object. However, the mirror is not faithful. There was a distortion of the image. The object, which was originally in the accusative, is now in the dative. The predicate, which in the original was simple, now comes with two ontologically problematic auxiliary verbs, the verbs *estar* (to be presently) and *ser* (to be essentially).[1] Let us also consider the following form, apparently intermediate, and possible, though rare, in Portuguese: *Há um escrever de um livro por mim* (There is the writing of a book by me). We now have three objects: *the writing, a book,* and *by me.* The predicate is there, and the subject has become invisible. We are, with these considerations, in the cradle of a problematic that

---

1 In Portuguese, the verb *to be* is ontologically divided into *ser,* which means Being in essence, as in *Eu sou o tradutor* (I *am* the translator), and *estar,* which means Being presently in a material sense, as in *Eu estou traduzindo* (I *am* translating). In English, this essential separation is not possible through language, hence the fundamental ontological difference between the concept of existence in the two languages. [T.N.]

accompanies the entire history of philosophy and also of theology. This problematic can be characterized by the words *subjectivity* and *objectivity,* on one hand, and *activity* and *passivity* (or *action* and *passion*), on the other. The religious ethical aspect of this problem appears best in the following example: *Beats me = I am being beaten = There is a beating upon me.* However, the first example is already problematic enough to serve as a basis for an analysis that should shed light on the maze of these problems.

The active form is *I am writing a book.* This phrase means a situation (a *Gestalt,* as some psychologists might say) composed of a center *(I)* radiating something *(writing)* toward a horizon *(a book)*. Something is transferred or being transferred from one substance (signified by the noun *I*) to another substance (signified by the noun *a book*). The passive form is *a book is being written by me.* The situation is reversed. Something is transferred or is being transferred from the horizon of the situation to the center. The subject absorbs the irradiation of the object. The intermediate form is *there is the writing of a book by me.* The situation now is that of a flux between two poles subordinated to an invisible center, namely, *what there is.* The confusion of traditional philosophy consists in identifying these three situations. For traditional philosophy, the three phrases mean *the same situation, the same reality.* In fact, if we accept this premise, by agreeing that the three sentences mean *the same thing,* the problem of subjectivity and objectivity and the problem of activity and passivity become impenetrable. What is this *reality in itself,* which the three sentences supposedly mean? It can neither be active, nor passive, nor intermediate but is *anterior* to these three forms and therefore inarticulable. Would it be foolish to ask what this reality is *objectively*? *Objectively* means *as an object.* However, as has been seen, the object becomes subject in the passive form. The object is the passive reflection of the subject, and vice versa. If I ask myself, *What is the objective situation of the phrase I am writing a book?* I ask, in fact, what is the phrase from which the phrase *I am writing a book* is an object? I am therefore the victim of a regression to infinity. For this reason, and for the reasons given in the first chapter of this work, it is necessary to abandon the concept of the *situation in itself* that the three sentences supposedly mean. One must accept, humbly, that these are three distinct situations, although somehow linked together. This abandonment of an unconscious metaphysical *(metalanguage)* will facilitate, in passing, the comprehension of some recent results of otherwise incomprehensible research in physics. I refer, for example, to the description of light as being undulatory and as being corpuscular. The question, *How are these phenomena objectively?* has no meaning. Physics is penetrating here deeply into the fabric of language, almost exposing its ontological structure, and in this specific case, the mathematical structure of the language of science.

Having abandoned the deaf and mute metaphysics that postulates a common meaning to the three sentences under study, we can attempt their comparative analysis. To do so, it is enough to translate them into a single language, for example, German. The three sentences in German would be *Ich schreibe ein Buch, Ein Buch wird durch mich geschrieben,* and *Es gibt ein Schreiben eines Buches durch mich,* that is, literally, *I write a book, A book is being written by me,* and *There is the writing of a book by me.* The active form is practically identical in both languages. The difference resides only in the subject *I,* who seems somewhat superfluous in Portuguese but is indispensable in German. However, the structural similarity of the two phrases is a consequence of the similarity of the respective structures and not of the *situation.* In Hebrew, for example, the phrase would be *N chvtv sfr = I scribe* (masc.) *book*; it would therefore have a different structure and would mean a different situation. In both English and German, therefore, the active form of the phrase means that it irradiates, from a center toward a horizon, that transfer of something from one substance to another, of which I have spoken earlier. The passive form, however, diverges in German from the Portuguese form. This divergence is revealing. Let us first analyze the Portuguese form: *Um livro está sendo escrito por mim* (A book is being written by me). At the center of the situation is the subject *(a book)*, whose predicate is a form of being *(is)*. This quality of being is qualified more accurately: *What is the book? Becoming.* This quality of being is again qualified: *What is the book otherwise? Written.* The object forms the horizon of this ontologically difficult situation: *by me.* We are therefore facing a situation that has been analyzed ad nauseam (the expression is very appropriate in this context) by existentialist philosophy. The subject *(a book)* absorbs, that is, reaches and overcomes, the object that is its instrument *(by me)* in the stages *is, being,* and *written.* Speaking existentially, *I* am the cause of the book (*Ding* and *Bedingung*), and as the book *overcomes me,* that is, as the book *is being written,* I *become the instrument (Zeug)* of the book, and *I witness (Bezeugen)* its *being written (Dasein).* No existentialist would, however, agree with this interpretation of the situation, since, for him, *I* overcome *the book*; it is *my instrument.* So why this divergence of interpretations? Because the existentialist, as a prisoner of the ontological structure of German and French, does not know the *experience* of the passive in Portuguese, and more especially, he does not know the verb *estar.* Not having this *experience,* that is, not being able to speak Portuguese, he cannot conceive of a situation in which the roles he reserves in *existing* and *being ready at hand* (*Dasein* and *Vorhandensein*) are inverted. However, this is precisely what happens in the Portuguese passive form. I will not analyze it, because it is not pertinent to the problem under study, the predicate *está sendo escrito* (is being written). Suffice it to say that in the passive Portuguese phrase, the subject absorbs the object that serves it as an instrument.

The corresponding German phrase is *Ein Buch wird durch mich geschrieben* (A book is being written by me) or . . . *von mir geschrieben* (written from me). At the center of the situation lies the subject *(a book)*, of which a form of being *(becoming)* is predicated. However, if we ask the question we asked in analyzing the Portuguese form, namely, *How does the book become?* we would have no answer. The question that arises in this case is, *What is the book becoming?* Answer: *Written. Where does the written book come from?* Answer: *From me.* The situation, then, is this: the object, which forms the horizon of the situation, is the place from where *(from me)* or where *(by me)* the subject appears; the object is the *humus* from which the subject springs. The subject is the effect of the object.

Let us compare the two situations. Both are centripetal, in the sense of the predicate process running from the horizon to the center. That is why we call them both passive. However, this similarity between the two *passivities* ends there. In the Portuguese type of passivity, the object is being absorbed by the subject; in the German one, the subject is being realized by the object. They are incongruent, almost contradictory types of passivity. Given this divergence of situations, given the radically different function of the subject in the Portuguese and German forms, it is understood that *object* and *subject* do not play the same role in the German and Portuguese structures. Therefore, when a German speaker speaks of *objectivity,* he forcibly thinks of something different from a Portuguese speaker, who uses the same Latin word. This problem requires patient analysis that far exceeds the scope of this work. I am convinced that this analysis will yield many problems of epistemology and of what passes for ontology today. The word *object,* for example, is translated into German as *Gegenstand.* However, this translation is the source of a multitude of misunderstandings. *Gegenstand* means passive *resistance.* The most accurate translation would be *Vorwent.* However, this word is translated into Portuguese as *recrimination* (that is, objection in the ethical sense). The coming and going of the translation between *object* and *Gegenstand* has, of course, reduced the distance that originally separated the two words, but the basic ontological difference persists. This is a single example of the work to be carried out by a future phenomenology of language in the field of logical analysis of phrases.

The intermediate form of the phrase under study is, in Portuguese, *Há um escrever de um livro por mim* (There is the writing of a book by me). This is a form against which the spirit of the language revolts. However, this is not an incorrect form and is therefore conceivable. The spirit of modern Indo-Germanic languages is contrary to indeterminate forms and allows them only when it is indispensable, as, for example, in the case *Há muita gente* (There are a lot of people). The Semitic languages, however, prefer these types of forms. The situation of this sentence is indeterminate, because the subject is hiding. Who is there? The question remains unanswered. The predicate of the original form has become an object *(a writing)*. It is therefore an objective situation to the extreme, because it consists of objects. What kind of objectivity is this? To what subject are these objects objected? The Portuguese language is silent about this respect, but the French language, a sister language, knows the answer. Who's there? *Il y a*. This is therefore an objectivity, which is, in effect, a transcendent subjectivity. But who is this *one there* who has the writing of the book for me? In order not to raise any doubt about it, it must be clarified that it is the neutral lost by the Latin languages. This neutral will be analyzed in one of the following sections.

The corresponding German form of the sentence under study is *Es gibt ein Schreiben eines Buches durch mich*. The two forms are very similar, except for the manifest presence of the neutral subject in German, and save the relation that this subject has to the objects. Whereas in Portuguese, the neutral subject possesses the objects, in German, it gives them. This difference, that is to say, both the manifest presence of the neutral subject and its relation to the world of objects, is, of course, fundamental, but it does not affect the problem we have discussed here, and I therefore relegate it to a future section. Both in the Portuguese and German forms, the objects are being aligned side by side *(the writing of a book by me)*. The difference between activity and passivity was overcome, and what was process became state. When we overcome the active and passive forms, we abandon the dynamic structure of the world, a structure required by the spirit of Indo-Germanic languages, and glimpse something of the static structure of the world, more appropriate, perhaps, to the Semitic languages. The phrase *Há um escrever de um livro por mim,* artificial as it may seem, serves, perhaps, as an introduction to a study of the Semitic languages.

If we compare the results of this research with the table of Aristotelian categories, we can state the following: the ontological structure of the modern Indo-Germanic languages does not allow a classification of their phrases according to the Aristotelian categorical system. This categorical system distinguishes between the accidents: action, passivity, relationship, and situation. The investigation of the three phrases showed that activity and passivity are a relation between object and subject, a relationship that is reversible according to the situation. In addition, the investigation revealed that there is a relationship that is neither active nor passive. I mention these circumstances not to argue against Aristotle but to illustrate that any category system not based on the grammar of a specific language is flawed not only ontologically (by presupposing an extra linguistic categorical reality) but also systematically (for being arbitrary in enumerating categories).

What the analysis of the three phrases revealed can be summed up as follows: the Portuguese and German languages (and, presumably, all the Indo-Germanic languages) have various modes of connection between subject, object, and predicate within the phrase. These modalities vary from language to language. However, given the similarity between Indo-Germanic languages, I can roughly say that the most usual of these modes of connection are the active and passive forms. Of course, since the links are different in each language, the meanings of *active* and *passive* from language to language also vary. Each connection mode means a different situation. *Passivity* is not, in the two languages analyzed (and presumably in no language), a reflection of *activity,* but it is a different situation, although consistent with approximately the same elements. *Batem-me* (they are beating me) does not mean an inverse situation to *Estou sendo batido* (I am being beaten) but a different situation. The tendency to say that it is the *same situation* is the result of a metaphysical faith in an ulterior meaning that had to be abandoned.

Subject and object have been revealed as being organs of phrases (presumably phrases of all Indo-Germanic languages); however, the function of these organs varies from language to language. The meanings of *subjective* and *objective* therefore vary according to language. Within the phrase, subject and object obey certain rules that vary from language to language and allow an approximate reversal of roles.

In short, *activity* and *passivity* are two modalities of phrase organization, preferred by Indo-Germanic languages, and are responsible for the dynamic character of Indo-Germanic *reality.* They are not, however, the only possible modalities. *Objectivity* and *subjectivity* are places reserved to certain words within Indo-Germanic phrases (perhaps within all the fusional languages). These places vary in importance, position, and function from language to language. Outside the field of fusional languages, the concepts of *activity, passivity, objectivity,* and *subjectivity* are meaningless.

A reinterpretation of the philosophical (and theological) discussion of the last four hundred years (that is, of the philosophical and theological discussion formulated in modern languages) should reveal that many basic problems are due to faulty translations of concepts related to the four concepts enumerated earlier. Let us consider, giving a single example, the function of the concept *opus* in the Catholic and Protestant theological systems and compare this function with the function of the concept *work* in the Marxist epistemological system. Of course, both concepts cover and include the basic concepts of *activity* and *object*. I am convinced that a phenomenological analysis of the thoughts of leading theologians and philosophers will reveal the hidden ontology that underlies them, namely, the ontology of the language within which they think, with the proper function for concepts such as *activity* and *object* within such ontology. Thus reinterpreted, all philosophical discussion will acquire a new meaning. This is a task for the future.

2.3. Substance

In Indo-Germanic languages (and presumably in all fusional languages), words called *nouns* are classified according to something called *gender*. According to traditional belief, nouns mean substances. It is surprising, therefore, that in the categorical systems, gender is not considered an accident. Perhaps the reason is the intimate connection between *substance* and *gender,* so that gender is subconsciously regarded as substantial, inseparable from essence. Fusional languages force us categorically to perceive the world of things as being divided into two (or three) categories. For the Portuguese language, we have, on one hand, things considered to be masculine, like *homem* (man), *pão* (bread), and *sol* (sun), and on the other side, things considered to be feminine, like *mulher* (woman), *natureza* (nature), and *lua* (moon). In German, man retains his place in the masculine: *der Mann*. And butter retains its feminine side: *die Butter*. The sun and the moon invert their places: *der Mond* and *die Sonne*. *Bread* and *woman* are relegated to a third neutral region, but certainly not genderless: *das Brot* and *das Weib*. These examples have been purposely chosen to stifle, at the outset, any hope that the reader may nurture in a correspondence between grammatical gender and the gender of the supposed *substance itself*. If, for example, in German, *das Weib* is neutral, the temptation is too strong to say that in this case, the language is *wrong*. In *reality* (we are tempted to say), the woman is female, whatever the grammatical form that designates her. If we analyze the situation, however, we will verify that *das Weib* does not mean *woman* and that the error is not in the language but in the translation. Within the ethical system of the German language, which in turn is a consequence of the ontological structure of that language, *das Weib* does not have the same gender as *die Frau*. For this ethical system, there are three genders, of which two are symmetrical (*der Mann* and *die Frau*) and one asymmetric *(das Weib)*. I have no doubt that much of the Lutheran sexual morality is influenced by the neutral *das Weib* as the *Gefäss der Suende* (the woman as the vessel of sin). Therefore, in this case also, we must abandon the concept of the woman *in herself,* although to do so is especially painful.

The division of the world of things into genders is therefore universal for fusional languages but varies from language to language. It is evident that this world of things has a radically different structure in a language with three genders than it has in Portuguese. This structure can be even more complicated than it first appears. In Czech, there are three genders: masculine, feminine, and neutral. The masculine and the feminine are, however, subdivided into animate and inanimate. Foreigners confuse these subdivisions and arouse in their interlocutor the feeling of a grotesque unreality (*kluky* instead of *kluci*), which proves that these subdivisions are felt to be part of reality. The division of the world into genders is therefore fundamental and prior to any further attempt at a division that our philosophy or science may undertake. However, mathematics, that universal language of fusional languages, seems to have overcome gender, seems to have desexualized the world of things. Symbols that replace nouns do not appear to have a gender. In its quest to overcome the divergences between the different ontological structures of fusional languages, mathematics seems to have succeeded in eliminating the gender of nouns. However, it seems to me that this success is merely apparent. Mathematical symbols do not mean *substances* but nouns of some fusional language. To mean substances, they need to be translated into nouns of some language. In the course of this translation, they regain gender. Mathematics reveals itself in this context as a kind of shorthand, in which, among other things, gender was omitted. To be read (that is, understood), however, mathematics needs to be rewritten in the original orthography, in which gender (and all other ontologically uncomfortable things) reappears.

These gendered nouns that pretend to mean substances are, as the words they are, organs of phrases. It is true that they have meaning even outside the phrase, and this characteristic precisely distinguishes fusional languages from agglutinative and isolating languages. As a result, there are no nouns in those types of languages. However, it is no less true that the noun acquires its full function only within a sentence. It becomes functional only as subject or object. *The noun* means, therefore, *a type of word apt to become subject or object of a phrase.* Or, thinking back to another layer of meaning, we are tempted to say, *substance means, therefore, a kind of phenomenon apt to become subject or object of a thought.* However, in view of the gender discussion about nouns we have just witnessed, we are forced to abandon the concept of *substance* as something *meant* by the noun. It would be far more appropriate to define *substance,* this first Aristotelian category, as what makes a word apt to become subject or object of a phrase according to the rules of the language in which the phrase must be formulated. *Substance* therefore requires gender in Portuguese and in Czech. In English, however, this demand for gender was reduced to a minimum.

The excursion into the gender of nouns became necessary to illustrate the purely formal aspect of the concept *substance.* This concept, or rather, its Greek ancestor *ousia* (verbally, "wood," "forest," "bush"), is responsible for much of the discussion called metaphysics in the Western tradition. *Substance, ousia,* was considered to be the basis of all transformations—the primordial amalgam formed by accidents, in short, the ultimate reality. Heated speculations have been exchanged as to the relationship of this *substance* with God. The mere fact of nouns having gender must, however, clarify how futile these speculations are. It should clarify that the concept *substance,* far from having any extralinguistic metaphysical meaning, is a formal element that enables the construction of phrases in the fusional languages.

With this consideration, the concept is not diminished in importance. Substance is an essential element of the phrase and therefore of thought, formulated in fusional languages. For us, there is no phrase, or thought, that does not have a substance as subject and object. However, it should be clear that this *ontological central role of the concept "substance"* varies from language to language.

The reader may object, in the hope of saving some *substantiality,* that the concept of *substance* is itself emphasized by our languages, because they distinguish nouns from other types of words. Yet this objection precisely strengthens the argument. Every word can be *substantive. O andar* (the walking) is the substantiation of a verb, or, to speak in an Aristotelian fashion, the category *action* passes to the *substance* category. *O juntar* (the joining) is the substantiation of a verb, which, in turn, is the verbalization of the adjective *junto,* or, to speak in an Aristotelian fashion, the category *relation* passes to the category *action* and from there to the category *substance.* The substantiation of words is possible in all fusional languages, but its method varies from language to language. A future phenomenology of grammatical forms will reveal, for example, the ontological meaning of the Portuguese suffix *-ade* (*bom = bondade*), the German suffix *-heit,* the Czech suffix *-nost,* and the pseudo-Latin suffix *-ism,* all of which are instruments of which the various languages take advantage in the process of substantiation.

In conclusion, I can say that *substance* is a criterion by which certain (fusional) languages organize the hierarchy of their words; that is, they confer on their words the dignity of acquiring the role (meaning) of subject or object in phrases (structures). Words acquire this dignity by methods that vary from language to language. This definition of substance brings, I believe, much of *metaphysical* speculation, the result of bad translations and a false interpretation of language, to an end.

2.4. Unity and Multiplicity

The purpose of this chapter is not, of course, to sift through the fabric of language with the hope to systematically discover all the elements that form its different structures. I intend only to suggest the direction in which, according to my opinion, a study must progress and submit to the reader some examples, taken at random, of superficial results of such a study. In this spirit, I propose that the problem of unity and multiplicity be considered at a glance. To do so, I propose the comparison by translation of the following structures: Portuguese, *uma mão, duas mãos, quatro mãos, cinco mãos*; English, *one hand, two hands, four hands, five hands*; Czech, *jedna ruka, dvě ruce, Čtyřruční, pět ruce*. In Portuguese, we can group these four structures into two different groups, according to the criterion of our choice: the first is in the singular, the other in the plural, or the first two have gender, whereas the others do not. In English, the division will be univocal: the first structure is in the singular, the others in the plural. In Czech, we cannot form authentic groups, because each structure is different: the first is in the singular and has gender; the second is in the dual and has gender; the third is in the plural, has no gender, and is ruled by the nominative; and the fourth is in the plural, has no gender, and is ruled by the genitive. What should we conclude from this comparison? That counting to five is a radically different process in the three languages under consideration. For English, reality is divided without problem into singular and plural and therefore into unity and multiplicity. For Portuguese, this division is comprehensible, but it does not articulate all of reality. In a way, the unit in Portuguese participates in substantiality; it has a gender, as the nouns do. Multiplicity, being genderless, is not substantive. However, *duality* does not yet plunge into the genderless insubstantiality of plurality; it still retains a gender. We therefore have, in Portuguese, the concept of substantial unity, the concept of substantial multiplicity (two), and the concept of insubstantial multiplicity (more than two). In Czech, the concept of unity is similar to that in Portuguese, although it has three genders instead of two. Multiplicity, however, is a concept that, as such, does not exist in Czech. We have organic duality, as in the case of *duas mãos,* which is a stage between unity and multiplicity. We have inorganic duality (two books), which resembles the Portuguese duality. And we have the multiplicity of *three* and *four,* which can be considered as organized multiplicity, although insubstantial. Czech considers the three and four as forms *(Gestalten).* We have, finally, the multiplicity of more than four, which is an amorphous multiplicity, of which quantity is a superficial aspect. To give an idea of this concept, I force a parallel with English: *There are fish in the ocean, five of which I caught.* This phrase gives a vague idea of Czech multiplicity.

What is the result of this discussion? Classical epistemology presupposes, with Kant, that *unity, multiplicity,* and *totality* are a priori categories of the human intellect. However, they are, as this discussion proves, categories of some languages. Other languages have different categories. And even in those languages that can be considered as having these categories (such as Portuguese), they can acquire different meanings. This is another illustration of how the structure of language produces *reality.*

2.5. Causality

Let us consider, for a moment, the concept of causality. Kant includes it among the categories of relation. Schopenhauer cancels all Kantian categories except causality. For him, causality is the only category of knowledge. The problem is considered basic at the present stage of the development of the natural sciences. The principle of causality is being abandoned by these sciences, and this leads to epistemological difficulties. What does an analysis of the language of this problem reveal? We will compare the following expressions: *por causa da chuva, devido à chuva, graças à chuva, wegen des Regens* (or *dem Regen*), *dank dem Regen, protože dešti*. The first three are Portuguese, the following two are German, and the last is Czech. They are approximately equivalent. However, despite participating nebulously in the category *causality,* all of them express relations that are irreducible to one another; they are incomparable to each other. The first expression, if analyzed, will reveal a strictly causal relation; it will be the authentic expression of the category *causality. The rain* will be the cause *by which* some effect will arise. Certainly the word *por* will create some difficulty, but it cannot be avoided, because it participates in the causal question *por quê?* (why?). The cause, within Portuguese causality, is not, therefore, the generator of the effect. The expression is *por causa de* and not *de causa de,* and the question is *por quê* and not *de que.* The cause is the channel through which the effect emerges. Let us, however, disregard this circumstance and say that Portuguese has a structure that expresses *causality.* German and Czech do not have comparable structures. *Durch Ursache des Regens, presprícinu dešte,* which would be literal translations of the Portuguese expression, would be constructions contrary to the spirit of the language and therefore difficult to think of. But even if they were accepted as valid (something unimaginable linguistically), they would not solve the problem. The Portuguese concept is lacking in these two languages, and the proposed translation distorts it. *Ursache* means primordial thing, something perhaps related to the *prima causa* of the ancient thinkers. *Príčina* means additional act, something perhaps related to the Aristotelian final causation. In short, the Portuguese concept of cause is lacking in German and in Czech, as much as the structure of causality.

We can make an effort to save *causality* in German (although we cannot do it in Czech) using the structure *Durch den Regen* (through rain). We will have thus saved something of the flavor of the Portuguese structure, but I do not think we have saved anything of *causality*.

However, Portuguese itself has structures that are categorical without being recognized as such philosophically, which therefore fall into the category of *causality*. *Devido a chuva* (due to the rain) is an ethical relationship, drawn from the world of the *do ut des* (I give that you might give), a relation that apparently characterized much of the *physis* of the Greeks. This means the *mutual payment of pain and retribution for injustice, according to the disposition of time,* in the famous phrasing of Anaximander. This is a relation that reappears in English with double strength—*due to*—but which is lacking both in German and in Czech. *Verschuldet dem Regen* has no meaning.

The other structure I proposed is *graças à chuva* (thanks to the rain). Far from me to want to analyze that enormous aura of meaning that covers the concept of *graça* (grace): *graça Divina* (Divine grace), *graça de uma menina* (the grace of a girl), *graça de uma piada* (a funny joke) are three examples of its extension. In any case, *graças à chuva* can be located in an ill-determined place within the structure of this aura of meaning. The concept of *graça* is, I believe, not translatable to any language. This is one of those words that characterize Portuguese. The structure under analysis is therefore sui generis and cannot be translated.

The structure *wegen des Regens* (formally correct) or *wegen dem*

Regen (idiomatically correct) says roughly *by the ways of the rain*, that is, *by the method of rain*. This is the expression of a genetic and not a causal relation, in fact, a relation that characterizes well the deep tendency of the German language toward biologization. There is no parallel relation in the Portuguese language. The structure *dank dem Regen* (grateful to the rain) is close but still far from *graças à chuva*, albeit in a completely different atmosphere. A patient analysis of these forms will certainly help to clarify the career of the concept of *causality*, so foreign to the spirit of the German language in the course of German philosophical conversation. For example, when Schopenhauer says that the Will has no foundation *(der Wille ist grundlos)*, this thought is untranslatable if taken seriously. What Schopenhauer tries to think about is the transcendence of the Will beyond the category of causality (*Grundlos* = unmotivated and therefore without cause). However, the category of causality characterizes, according to Schopenhauer, *the world of representation (Vorstellung)*. What Schopenhauer tries to think about is that this world *covers (stellt sich vor)* the Will, or rather, it covers our view of the Will. Causality is a consequence of this blinded view. This imaginary category, covering and representing the Will at the same time, thus presents it to our imagination. All that I have just said is an attempt to translate *Vorstellung*. It would be necessary to analyze what type of causality Schopenhauer thinks when he opposes it to the unfounded *(grundlos)*: whether it is the causality of *wegen* or of *dank*. Another example: Kelsen, in his *Vergeltung und Kausalität,* proposes a theory by which the world is transformed, with the progress of civilization, from society into nature, from partner into instrument, from *you* into *it*. In the course of this transformation, the field of *retribution* is restricted (it must be noted that in German, *Vergeltung* also means *revenge*), and the field of causality is increased. The book quoted is, I believe, a basic work of a contemporary philosophy of law. All that Kelsen seems to want to think about is the transition from *dank* to *wegen*. Causality is not exactly what he is elaborating in contrast to *Vergeltung* but precisely this typically German relation *wegen*.

Let us consider, finally, the *pro déšť* structure (in favor but also in exchange—of rain). As always, Czech reveals, as a language a little more distant, an aspect of the problem that almost cannot be framed in the set of examples. The articulated relation in the Czech form seems to have nothing in common with the concept of causality. I will not analyze this relationship; I will only say that it sees the causal nexus as a *post hoc, ergo propter hoc* and at the same time moralizes such a nexus.

What is the result of this discussion of the problems that come together, in the three languages considered, around and close to the category called *causality*? I think I can put it this way: causality, far from being a category of pure reason, is a category of some languages. Other languages do not know this category. Moreover, languages are rich in different types of relations, characteristic of their respective structures, and these relations are generally untranslatable.

2.6. Being

So far I have proposed structures (grammatical forms) for the reader's consideration. Now I suggest that some words (concepts) be considered as well. I will start by considering a hybrid phenomenon of some languages, something between grammatical form and word, between structure and concept: the Portuguese *há*, the English *there is*, the German *es gibt*, and the Hebrew *yesh*. The Portuguese expression is the third person of the lost neutral of the archaic verb *haver* and has at least two meanings: *Há gente na sala* (There are people in the room) and *há dois anos* (two years ago). With regret, I shall set aside the second meaning, for it is not pertinent in this context. This first form of the past has been discussed previously as producing the neutral form between the active and passive forms, which is an amorphous and

ontologically problematic statement of what traditional (not existential) philosophy calls *existence*. The phrase *há gente* affirms the
existence *of these people in the room*. Verbally, however, the phrase
says, *The lost neutral (it) has people*. The Portuguese language,
therefore, defines existence as the property of *it*. In the French
form, *il y a,* this definition becomes more explicit. The situation
is complicated, however, by the appearance of the word *y* (there).
There are people in the room. A comparison with the English language makes it clear that the word *y* (there) should not be interpreted as indicating a place *(There they are—or there are—people
in the room)*. Where? In *the room* and not *there*. It is evident that
the English *there* is equivalent to the French *il y a* and to the now
lost Portuguese *aquilo aí*. What is this neutral? In the Portuguese
language, the neutral is the foundation of existence, being the
owner of it. In the English language, the neutral is the foundation
of existence that transcends it *(there is)*. In the German language,
the neutral is the foundation of existence, being the giver of it *(es
gibt)*. In this amorphous and imprecise neutral, which is difficult
to grasp, the languages under study are close to an articulation
of the inarticulable. These are three different concepts of what
Kierkegaard called *the all different*.

The forms at which we are looking seem to want to disorganize
the basically logical fabric of their languages. They are like wedges
inserted in this fabric. They do not seem logically analyzable. It is
for this reason that I refer exceptionally to the example of a non-
Indo-Germanic language, in the hope of illuminating the situation
of our languages from the outside.

Hebrew is a language that has neither the verb *to be* nor the
verb *haver* nor the present of any verb. I do not dare to analyze the
ontological meaning of these characteristics of Hebrew, because,
not participating in the Hebrew conversation, that language does
not form my intellect. I cannot, therefore, attempt this by the introspective method. I do, however, feel that the reality of Hebrew

must necessarily be fundamentally different from our own. Well, although Hebrew has neither the verb *to be* nor the verb *haver* nor the present of any verb, it has the word *yesh,* which is translated as meaning *there is,* and if accompanied by the dative (*yesh li* = there is me), as *I have.* This *yesh* is the only grammatical form of the present in the Hebrew language. Although the concept of the *present* is probably simply lacking in Hebrew, and, despite the concept of time in Hebrew being radically different from ours, this *yesh* form—being altogether exceptional within the Hebrew fabric—must have an exceptional ontological meaning. I will tentatively point out that the Hebrew language overcomes, in the word *yesh,* time in the Hebrew sense, thus expressing something that it is normally incapable of articulating: *Being* and *its property.*

Despite its exceptional position within the language, the word *yesh* is one of the most used. It is not a word of holy meaning. This is necessary to emphasize in the case of a language so saturated with holiness as Hebrew. *Yesh* is a word of the conversational layer of that language.

In what way can the contemplation of the word *yesh* clarify the problem of *há, there is,* and *es gibt*? I think we can say, at least hypothetically, that these forms represent an archaism of languages, a kind of remembrance of the stage during which language did not yet have the verb *to be.* The hypothesis would be similar to those hypotheses of comparative anatomy, which establish parallels between, for example, fish gills and mammalian ears. In our hypothesis, Hebrew would serve as fish for modern mammals, which are the three Indo-Germanic languages under study. According to this hypothesis, as these languages deepened and developed their ontological capacity, the *yesh* of the ancient languages developed, in modern languages, into the various types of the verb *to be.* In the meantime, beside this development, the form *há* has been preserved as a not perfectly integrated archaism. *Há* serves, therefore, as a window that opens to a vision of an old and overcome ontology of language.

I dare not insist on the validity of this hypothesis. It needs to be investigated by a future science of language, in the sense outlined here. It seems, however, that this investigation will undoubtedly reveal a basic aspect of the languages studied: the fact that the Portuguese amorphous neutral *has (há)*, the English amorphous neutral *is at (there is)*, and the German amorphous neutral *gives (es gibt)* must be of fundamental importance for the appreciation of the hidden ontology in each of these languages.

Let us then consider the developed and modern form of the concept *há,* namely, the German verb *sein* and its most common translations into Portuguese: *ser, estar,* and *ficar.* We can dispense with, in this quick consideration, a comparison with other languages, although this comparison would certainly be very elucidating.

The verb *sein* has been subjected to a detailed analysis in the field of philosophical conversation for more than fifty years. This is, in fact, one of the few words being investigated in the sense proposed here. Since philosophical interest has again shifted toward ontology, that is, with N. Hartmann *(Zur Grundlegung der Ontologie)* and M. Heidegger *(Sein und Zeit),* the German word *sein* has been dissected with scalpels by the sharpest intellects. The German language, with its agglutinative tendency, lends itself exceptionally well to the formation of superwords that contain the *sein* nucleus and illuminate the extent of *sein*'s meaning. It is impossible to mention, even superficially, all these formations, because this would be tantamount to sketching out the entire ontology of the present time. I will evidence, for the contemplation of the reader, only the forms that seem to me to be the most characteristic. *Ansichsein* and *Fürmichsein* (Hartmann) ("being-as-such" and "being-for-me") are the attempt to base the relation between *subject* and *object* ontologically. Hartman confesses that this difference merges into *schlechthin Seiendes* (absolutely being), but Sartre, who does not have the immediate experience of the German words, translates them to *être en soi* and *être pour moi* and arrives at a different result. For Sartre (who thinks inauthentic, translated words), *être en soi* is the mode of being of everything but man. It is a modality full of itself *(trop plein)*, which provokes nausea when contemplated *(nausée)*, unless the one who contemplates it is *swinish (salaud)*. The *être pour moi* is the human mode of being, which is more empty, as nothingness has invaded it. It is a problematic modality and represents, in this sense, a victory for nothingness. The difference between Hartmann and Sartre is the difference between the original and the translation. *Ansichsein* does not provoke the nausea of the *être en soi* because *en soi* is *an sich,* but also *in sich.* As a consequence, Sartre arrives at an ontological distinction between *être en soi* and *être pour moi* that is impossible for Hartmann. The Sartrean position, with *man* in the center, is possibly a fruitful consequence of this mistranslation.

Dasein, Sosein, Vorhandensein, and *Zuhandensein* (Heidegger) ("being-here," "being-thus," "being-at-hand," and "being-to-hand")— it is important to note that these words, though used in a new context by Heidegger, are not artificial but authentic within the fabric of the German language. His is an analysis of the various modalities of Being, which we can visualize, in Portuguese, approximately in the following way: *Dasein* is what exists effectively, that is, what acts. *Sosein* is the essence of *Dasein*; it is that which is here to act *(Da).* *Vorhandensein* is the mode of being on which *Dasein* can act and thus determines *Dasein.* This is the mode of Being of things. *Zuhandensein* is the mode of Being that demonstrates, witnesses, the activity of *Dasein* and attests, therefore, the *Sosein* of *Dasein.* This is the mode of Being of instruments.

Wesen, Anwesenheit, and *Verwesung* (their normal translations are "Being," "presence," and "decomposition"; formally, they translate as "have been," "have-been-togetherness," and "unbeingness"). The first word, which is the defective past participle of the verb *sein,* is of prime importance in German thought and, by erroneous translation, in the thinking of the West. *Wesen* is translated as *Being,* as *essence,* and, according to Husserl, as *eidos.* But it always retains the flavor of the past, of the overcome. This is perfect Being, in the sense of *already done.* Husserlian phenomenology established the *eidetic* sciences, which put in parentheses all the existential aspects of Being, to liberate the *Wesen.* I have no doubt that a phenomenological analysis of the word *Wesen* will liberate *Wesen.*

The word *Anwesenheit* (presence) and the word *Verwesung* (decomposition, putrefaction, rot) are, for those who feel the spirit of the German language, modalities of *Wesen.* As we do not yet have an *essentialist* philosophy parallel to *existentialism,* these words have not been analyzed with the same patience as the formations of *sein* have. This is a gap that the future will have to fill.

Those who analyze the derivatives of the word *sein*—in other words, the whole current of ontological thought called existentialism, phenomenology, and the Marburg School—almost glimpse the linguistic aspect of this analysis. Jaspers says that the ancients could not have developed an authentic ontology because they conceived phrases such as *hic leo (hier ist ein Loewe).* The example is unfortunate, because in Portuguese, the phrase is *aqui está o leão,* and not *aqui é o leão.* But I will deal with this aspect later. Jaspers comes close to formulating the fact that ontology is a consequence of language. What he does not know, as he ignores the multiplicity of languages, is that this ontology will be different from language to language. In Czech, the Latin form still persists (*hic leo = zde lev*). And Cassirer, of the Marburg School, develops a neo-Kantianism that expressly considers *language as the form of thought.* Evidently, *thought* and *reality* are identical for this current. However, as he despises the multiplicity of languages, Cassirer does not come to a linguistic reinterpretation of ontology either.

The translation of the word *sein* into Portuguese radically reveals this linguistic dependence of ontology. The Portuguese language analyzes the diverse modalities of *sein* without existentialism, without phenomenology, and without the categorial analysis of Hartmann. Heidegger, Jaspers, Sartre, and Camus might have analyzed the problem of Being in a radically different way had they learned Portuguese. The word *ser* means roughly the *Sosein* of the existentialists (being-thus), the word *estar* stands largely for *Dasein* (being-here), and the word *ficar* encompasses *Vorhandensein* and *Zuhandensein* ("being-at-hand" and "being-on-hand"), even surpassing them. *O prédio fica do lado direito* (the building *is/stands* on the right side) signifies both its availability and the limitation it represents for those on the street, that is, for those who are *(são)* pedestrians. The simple contrast of these three Portuguese words in this context clarifies, in one blow, the problematic of existentialism and is worth several readings on philosophical themes. Thinkers such as Hartmann and Heidegger, who strive honestly to exceed the limits imposed on them by the German language, could never come to formulate the modes of Being as authentically as the Portuguese language does. Portuguese is a fundamentally *existential* language, while German tends to the *essential,* as in *Wesen.* It is a paradox of our generation that modern existentialism emerged within the German conversation.

In short, I can formulate the result of this section as follows: every language has structures and concepts to signify *reality.* For example, the German language does it with the verb *sein* and the Portuguese with the verbs *ser, estar,* and *ficar.* Latin can dispense with the verb and articulate reality with the structure of the sentence as does Czech: *hic leo = zde lev.* Hebrew has no verb or structure meaning *reality,* but it has the form *yesh,* which is parallel to *há, there is,* and *es gibt. Reality* is, therefore, something different from language to language. Even through a superficial analysis of some words of ontological meaning, one of the fundamental theses of this work has been proven, so to speak, experientially. I shall try to expand this experiential demonstration in the course of this chapter.

2.7. Potentiality

I invite you to consider with me the concept that surrounds reality, the concept of which reality is the realized nucleus, the Portuguese concept of *poder* (power). Potentiality is reality in statu nascendi, or, to speak technically, the increased potency of necessity results in reality. The verb *poder* means, therefore, almost exactly what Heidegger tries to think by saying that *nothingness nullifies. Poder* means *non-being tending toward Being. Poder,* as a noun, clearly demonstrates that it is a dynamic concept, which admits increases and decreases. Something has either *more or less potency*; has greater or lesser power; is either closer to or farther from reality. The noun *poder* is the substantiation of nothingness in its progress toward realization. Reality is total power, perfect power. The concept is that of a Darwinian struggle for power; it is the pressure of nothingness toward Being—the nullifying species want to come to power, to become realized. Reality is the spearhead of power: what is *is* because it could be. *Não pode* (it cannot) is a ban on realization; also, in an ethical sense, it means it *should not* become. *Power (poder)* and *duty (dever)* are connected concepts, and I am sure that a phenomenological study of the two words will fundamentally clarify the ontological system that supports the Portuguese language. It will reveal, as I believe, a tendency of this language toward fatalism (duty = power).

The translation of the word *poder* into English turns out to be of unsurpassed ambiguity. *Posso fazer* is translated as *I may do, I can do, I am able to do,* and *I am allowed to do.* All of these phrases have a different meaning. Of course, the concept *poder* is missing in the English language. The concept of *potentiality* is employed by English philosophy, but in its Latin and scholarly form. It does not integrate authentically into the fabric of the English language. English thought revolves in different regions when it seeks *Being* in order to distinguish it from *nothingness.* These regions are characterized by concepts such as *happen* (by chance), *get* (get to, become, beget, forget, overcome, and realize), and *Will* (to want, but see also the section about time). The central ontological word seems to me to be *get,* which seems to encompass both the region of the possible and that of the realized, but in an inconceivable way to the Portuguese intellect. I do not know if *get* has an etymological link with *Wesen;* if "g" is equivalent to "w" and "t" to "s," this may be possible. To condense in a single sentence what I believe to be the fundamental tendency of the English language, I would say, *To get at what will happen* (to reach that which wants to become realized, thus it shall be realized). There is no vacant space in such an ontology for concepts like *poder* and *ser.* In fact, the concept of *ser* is almost as untranslatable as the concept of *poder.*

The translation of *poder* into German strikes against difficulties of another kind. Two translations are insistently offered: *können* and *mögen.* The others, such as *dürfen* and *vermögen,* though probably as important as the former, will not be considered. *Können* means power in the sense of *knowing* (to do), and *mögen* means power in the sense of *wanting* (to do). It is clear that both concepts fail to translate the Portuguese *poder,* which is not necessarily a *power to do.* Let us first consider the word *mögen.* It comes from the same family as the word *machen* (to make) and forms the concepts *möglich* (possible) and *Macht* (substantive power). However, *mögen* means *to want, to like, to love.* It is in this context of *mögen* that we must locate Nietzschean ontology; the *Wille zur Macht* (Will to Power), *amor fati,* in short, this whole set of thoughts that caused today's philosophy. This type of *mögen* potentiality is responsible, among other things, for the concept of the Freudian *subconscious;* it is the libido wanting to become realized: the dynamization of erotics, on one hand, and the sexualization of potentiality, on the other, the enthronement of sexual potency as the driving power of the intellect, is the result of an unconscious Freudian analysis of *mögen* as a concept. Psychoanalysis is not an analysis of *intellectual reality,* but of *intellectual possibility,* that is, an analysis of *mögen.*

Let us now consider the word *können.* Its noun is *Kunst,* translated as *art.* The reality that is realized from this potentiality is the artwork. It is in this context that we must place the Nietzschean phrase *Art is better than truth.* With this thought Nietzsche seeks to overturn what he calls *Platonism,* which he identifies with *truth.* *Truth,* for Nietzsche, is the Platonic affirmation of a correspondence between the world of appearances and the world of ideas. For Nietzsche, the world of ideas is nothing, and therefore Plato is a nihilist. Reality, by contrast, emerges through art. Therefore *art is better than truth.* However, what Nietzschean thought really means is, in my opinion, to replace the Latin concept of *potentiality* that has dominated all of Western philosophy since the Middle Ages (and which Nietzsche identifies with *Platonism*) by the German *können.* Nietzsche's effort, then, is basically the effort to translate *poder* into German. This is a good example of the productivity of translation, even when it is unconscious, as in Nietzsche's case.

At this point in the argument, I want to introduce a small aside. I submit to the reader's appreciation the following: the traditional philosophy of the West apparently offers no difficulties in linguistic interpretation up until the seventeenth century: this philosophy is Latin. It is true that this is an artificial Latin, superimposed on the author's mother tongue as a cloak. A study of the Latin of Duns Scotus would probably reveal, for example, its Scottish influences, or one of Spinoza's Latin the influences of his Sephardic Portuguese. However, the linguistic difficulty of the philosophical tradition has lain masked. From the seventeenth century, the philosophy of modern languages begins through the practice of neo-Latin, English, and German languages. The neo-Latin ones easily adapted to the Latin concepts and did not feel the difficulty of deep translation. But English and German thought had to make an ongoing translational effort to continue the Western conversation. English philosophy, and even more the German one, is fruit of that effort. The originality, wealth, and productivity of these two philosophies are due to the new thoughts that are formulated when Latin thoughts are translated into such distant languages. Now the process begins to reverse. The neo-Latin (and Slavic) languages must strive to translate English and German concepts and constructions into their own structures.

Summing up the argument, the place that *poder* occupies in the structure of Portuguese finds at least two possibilities in the structure of German: *mögen* and *können*. Both, however, cannot completely fill it. To do so, it is necessary to include the concept of *werden*, which has already been slightly discussed. To grasp something of the meaning of German speculation as to the regions before *Being*, that is, as to *potentiality*, as to *nothingness*, as to *anguish*, as to the *Will*, and finally as to the emerging of *reality*, we must try to understand the concepts *mögen*, *Köennen*, and *werden*. Concluding this section, I can say the following: *potentiality*, like *reality*, is a concept whose meaning depends on the language in which I think.

2.8. *Es*

To illustrate with more emphasis this thesis, which is basic to the present work, I draw attention to the sui generis function that the word *es* plays in the structure of the German language. The *es gibt* form has already been discussed. Therefore I propose the forms *es erhellt daraus* and *es füllt sich der Raum* (approximately, "it is evident" and "it fills the space"). Finally, the form *es strahlt aus der Sonne* (it radiates from the sun). My purpose is to point to a language horizon that will be of importance in the argument that will be developed in the next chapter.

In the first two forms proposed, the *es* is apparently superfluous. I can say, without changing the meaning, *daraus erhellt* and *der Raum füllt sich*. Likewise, the two seemingly superfluous *es* are not entirely identical. The first *es* corresponds vaguely to the

Portuguese *se*; it is the vaguely logical subject of the phrase. Who
concludes this? It. *(Wer erhellt daraus? Es.)* That type of *es* could
be replaced, to a certain extent, by the word *Man* (*Man erhellt
daraus* = We have concluded this). In the second example, the
es does not correspond to any Portuguese concept. *Se enche-se o
espaço* is inconceivable in Portuguese. In the third example, the *es*
apparently seems to approximate the Portuguese *algo* (something):
algo irradia os raios a partir do sol (something radiates the rays from
the sun). But the Portuguese phrase thus formulated presupposes
something real that radiates the rays from the sun; the German
phrase, of a completely different climate, leaves the subject at a
nebulous and logically unreachable distance. The German translation of this new Portuguese phrase would be *etwas strahlt aus
der Sonne,* which gives the German phrase a completely different
meaning from the proposed phrase. We have, therefore, at least
four types of *es*: (1) the superfluous *es,* vaguely meaning *se*; (2) the
superfluous *es* having no Portuguese equivalent; (3) the irreplaceable *es,* vaguely resembling *algo*; and (4) the *es* signifying the lost
Portuguese neutral within *há.*

Those who have researched the nebulous regions from which
the intellect has condensed and into which it will immerse itself
are not, in this case, practicing philosophical thought *sensu stricto*
but so-called *depth psychology.* Freud, and later C. G. Jung, penetrate
with their thoughts the regions that are intellectually so difficult
to access and call them *es,* a word that is translated in this context as *id.* Our superficial analysis of the word reveals, however,
how ambiguous the concept is. The *id* of depth psychology, while
ontologically significant, is not a mature concept. It is necessary
patiently to elaborate this meaning, which undoubtedly points to
the horizon of language.

The two types of replaceable *es* point to a quality of language
that stands out as a foreign body in this context. The presence of *es,*
although logically superfluous, confers a poetic quality to language.

The *es* that can be loosely translated as *se* points to a prelinguistic region that was analyzed by existential thought and denominated as *man,* or *on,* that is, *a gente* (one/we). The *irreplaceable es* points to the inarticulable region that it articulates. In short, the *es* that hides behind *há* points to a region of the inarticulate that language tends to articulate. All these considerations will become clearer when we reach the third chapter of this work. These considerations are placed in this context because they refer to the structure of language, yet they are thematically premature.

2.9. Portuguese as an Investigation Tool

In the course of this chapter, I was constantly surrounded by the entanglement of wealth. The fabric of language is like human life: *Wo Ihr's packt, da ist's interessant* (Wherever you grasp it, there it becomes interesting). I felt like an explorer in the middle of an archipelago of thousands and thousands of islands, each one more beautiful and inviting, more beautiful and mysterious in its own way. It was unfortunately not possible to visit or glimpse more than an insignificant fraction of the islands. The others are still there, easily accessible, waiting to be discovered. Who knows what treasures they hide?

I followed a path in the midst of this richness: I chose the Portuguese language as the background of two or three others, namely, English, German, and Czech. The greatest emphasis was given to German for three reasons: (1) German is sufficiently far removed from Portuguese to create different concepts and structures, but close enough to make them usable to the Portuguese intellect; (2) German is independent, to a degree more intense than English, of concepts formed by the Latin language; (3) German is almost my mother tongue. The Czech, of which I have perhaps a more immediate experience, is too different from Portuguese, and English is too Latinized.

I have made to resonate, within this Portuguese base, through the method of translation and retranslation, a few grammatical structures and very few concepts of the three guinea pig languages. The purpose was to illustrate how strange and distorted, in a word, unreal, these structures and these concepts sound within the Portuguese set. For this I chose structures and concepts usually considered independent of language, namely, categories considered by the philosophical tradition to be universally human and concepts considered as signifiers of absolute reality. The reader will judge whether I have been able to demonstrate their dependence on language.

Problems emerged in the course of the development of the argument that are part of the philosophical discussion of current times. This was normal, because if the argument is correct, these problems are fundamentally linguistic. These problems have been, therefore, welcomed with hospitality and developed within the general tenet of the argument. It is my hope that some of them have been clarified with a new light or presented in a new angle.

The goal of this chapter, as formulated at the end of the previous chapter, has been achieved only in part. I proposed to verify that philosophical and scientific research is ultimately an investigation of language. Perhaps I have made this statement plausible in relation to philosophy. However, I did not fulfill the task in relation to science. In the following chapters of this work, I will investigate the role of science.

Conclusion

I will summarize the result achieved so far: the fusional languages that make up the conversation that results in Western civilization differ in terms of their elements (words: concepts) and their structure (rules and types of phrases: thoughts). But all these structures are of the same type, namely, phrases are composed of relatively constant but flexible and hierarchically organized words. Consequently, concepts (words) and thoughts (phrases) are different from language to language but can be compared to each other. There is, in this sense, the possibility of translation and therefore the possibility of conversation between languages, which is the origin of Western civilization.

This possibility of translation reveals that each structure of each individual language corresponds to a different meaningful cosmos. Each language is a different world; each language is the whole world and different from any other language. This paradox is solved if we consider that each language includes in its world all other languages through translation. The intellect, realized in the conversation of a specific language, apprehends, comprehends, and articulates the specific reality of its language. Through the method of translation, one can participate in different realities. Reflecting on this method, that is, by conversing conversation and translation, the intellect can compare the different realities. This is the role of philosophy. In fact, this is what philosophy has always done, but it has done so more or less unconsciously. Self-conscious philosophy will be the conversation of conscious conversation.

Language, with its structure and its concepts, is a superorganization, which is composed of languages. Intellects participate in language, participating in one or more specific languages. They can never therefore have a full comprehension of *language*. In the rest of this work, a full view of language will be attempted, always keeping in mind the limitation of the intellect to one or a few specific languages.

From now on, therefore, the Portuguese language will be used as an instrument to perform, that is, to articulate, *language* in Portuguese words and phrases. An abstraction of the diversity of languages will therefore be made. The reader should constantly fill this vacuum left by such abstraction if he or she wants to achieve the vision of language being sketched here. Unfortunately, abstraction is necessary, because it is not possible to think or write a book simultaneously in several languages.

3

LANGUAGE CREATES REALITY

See The Physiology of Language graph [appendix]. In the first two parts of this work, I sought to put together arguments and illustrations in favor of the fundamental hypothesis that I can now formulate in the following way—the unreal chaos of becoming, of coming-to-being, and of potentiality that tends to become realized, which we are accustomed to call *reality,* emerges, appears to the intellect, and organizes itself into a cosmos; in sum, it becomes realized in the form of the various languages. Conversely, the unreal chaos of becoming, that set of potentialities we are accustomed to referring to as instincts, inarticulate experiences, and sensorial impressions—in sum, *the subconscious*—emerges, organizes itself, becomes intellect, and objectifies itself, that is, it becomes realized, in the form of the various languages. In other words, the various languages are the forms in which the potentialities of the Self and the Non-Self are realized, or the Self and the Non-Self are the ontological horizons (the borderline situations) of language as a whole. This fundamental hypothesis has as an immediate consequence the elimination of the Self and the Non-Self from the territory of all discussion, because they are both extralinguistic *ex hypothese* and therefore nondiscussable. However, because they are both horizons of language, they are both what the discussion tends toward. The

Self and the Non-Self, precisely because they are extralinguistic, are the nondiscussable goal toward which the discussion (which is the set of languages) expands. The Self and the Non-Self are the two faces of that *nothingness* that, according to existential thought, *establishes (Herstellt)* Being. The following situation arises: the set of languages, this set of realized potentials, emerges from the nothingness of the Self and Non-Self and expands toward the same nothingness. It has its origin in nothingness and seeks this nothing. The great conversation in which we participate, and which is reality as a whole, comes from nothingness and is about nothingness. But this affirmation no longer has, at this point in the discussion, any taste of defeat or despair. Nothingness, far from being an empty and negative concept, becomes a superconcept, synonymous with the unutterable. Reformulating, therefore, we can say that the great conversation we are emerges from the unutterable and is about the unutterable. I believe that with this phrase, the territory of language has been delimited. This phrase, which is an attempt to formulate a thought that is almost no longer thought, this phrase which tends to overcome itself, annihilating itself in this attempt, seems to be paradoxical in itself, on one side, and tautological, on the other. That the conversation comes from the unutterable and is about the unutterable seems paradoxical because this seems to say that the conversation discusses the nondiscussable. And the phrase seems tautological because it seems to say that conversation means something beyond itself, namely, *meaning.* However, as the unutterable is *synonymous with nothingness,* the paradox and apparent tautology of the phrase dissolve. To those who follow the argument attentively and patiently, it must have become clear that its two poles, among which it oscillates, are precisely paradox and tautology. Necessarily, because this is an argument that vibrates between the two horizons of language. Clashing against one, it becomes seemingly paradoxical, and then it comes back and collides with the other, making itself seemingly tautological. Yet, in the process of oscillation, the argument progresses. The preceding phrase represents the limit of this progress. Being at once seemingly paradoxical and tautological, the phrase expresses, as I believe, what is closest to a definition of both language and reality. I want to devote the rest of this work to an analysis of that phrase.

I repeat: the great conversation that we are, and that is reality as a whole, has emerged and always emerges from the unutterable, from nothingness, and tends toward (that is, it means) the unutterable and nothingness. That nothingness, the unutterable, which is therefore the Alpha and the Omega of conversation, tries, in the course of the conversation, to infiltrate itself and to articulate itself, a task that is *ex definitione* impossible. It is in this sense that we must interpret Wittgenstein's statement that the history of human thought is the collection of bruises that this thought accumulated as it precipitated itself against the borders of language. During this attempt of infiltration, nothingness acquires several names. *Objectively,* it is called the *thing-in-itself, all-different,* and *Non-Self. Subjectively,* it is called *spirit, subject,* and *Self.* These are attempts to name the inarticulable. These attempts are responsible for the so-called *eternal problems* of thought: eternal because they are insoluble. To be able to distinguish the sayable from the unsayable is one of the advantages of the platform that we have climbed upon with our phrase. Thus we delimit the territory of the discussion; we attribute to discursive reason a limited, though expanding, region. And we recognize regions that, although progressively penetrated by discursive reason (as language expands), are not yet, and perhaps never will be, in their totality, discursive. These regions, being anterior or posterior to language, are unreal, are nothingness. But it is this unreality, this nothingness, that establishes reality, and in this sense, this unreality is more basic, or superior, in relation to reality. As it becomes realized in language, the intellect loses that unreality superior to reality and seeks to reconquer it by overcoming language. However, since realized *intellect* is only a *subjective* name for language, we must say that language, as a whole, is a process of realization that tends to overcome itself. Language, this realization of potential, expands toward the supra-real and ceases to be language in this advance. The amorphous shutting off of potentiality, from which language emerges, gives way to the superconcentration of indiscoursability, in which language loses itself. These are two different types of silence, although they both mean *nothingness*. This is, on one hand, the silence of the not yet articulated, the silence of the animal and the cretin, and, on the other hand, the silence of the no longer articulable, the silence of St. Thomas, Wittgenstein, and the Buddha. If we look at language as a process of realization, we must see it as something that condenses gradually, from the animalesque silence, to evaporate again, within the supraintellectual silence. The stages of this condensation and evaporation are observable. From the first infant or idiotic babble to the last Sibyl-like or supersymbolic babble, language can be followed and observed. This is not, however, a simple and easily interpreted process. This is not a well-defined, unilinear process. The evaporation of language into the supra-real is processed in several directions and loses itself in various nothingnesses. The silence of Wittgenstein is different from the silence of the Buddha. The babbling of a mystagogue is different from the babbling of Moses. The supersymbolism of the mystics is different from the supersymbolism of mathematicians. The pure structure, signifying nothingness, that is modern painting's attempt to overcome language is different from the pure structure of the attempt done by logico-symbolic analysis to overcome language. Language expands in different directions and tends to be overcome in different ways. The failures of these attempts are also just as different. Inauthentic art, false mysticism, the false symbolism of an artificial mythology, and the word salad of demagoguery and madness are different forms of frustrated attempts. The difficulty resides in distinguishing between these various phases of language. This is what I will try to do in this chapter.

The first chapter of this work can be considered as an attempt to crosscut through language, uncovering the various languages and establishing the relationships between them. The second chapter can be considered as an attempt to discover the structure of language, exposing its skeleton. The third chapter will be an attempt to make a vertical cut through language, exposing its growth. To borrow biological concepts, I could say that the first chapter is an attempt at a morphology of languages, the second an attempt at an anatomy of languages, and the third an attempt at a physiology of languages. With this parallel in mind, I offer the reader the attached graphic. The south pole of this graph represents the transition from language to unreality. The equator represents what we normally call conversation; it is the center of language and the intermediate stage between the two unrealities. The climate of the southern hemisphere is the climate of *the people (man)*, in the existential sense, which is a climate of inauthenticity that progresses toward the pole. The climate of the northern hemisphere is the climate of *it (es)*, in the existential sense, which is a climate of authenticity that progresses toward the pole. The axis joining the two poles is the line along which language projects itself from authentic silence, or vice versa, along which language decays in the direction of inauthentic silence. The different climatic zones are attempts to represent several layers of language. The center of the graph represents language sensu stricto, that is, the set of symbols called, in the territory of fusional languages, *words*. The Far East represents the world of fundamentally auditory symbols, therefore, *music*. The Far West represents the world of fundamentally pictorial symbols, therefore, *the visual arts*. These concepts must be understood within quotation marks. On the whole, the graph represents language sensu lato. Of course, the graph is a Mercator projection; it represents a globe. *Music* and *the visual arts* are on the back of the graph. I urge the reader not to regard the graph as an attempt to illustrate reality but merely as an attempt to illustrate the progress of the argument in this chapter. It is intended as a graphic index of the chapter. Furthermore, if it can bring about new associations in the mind of the reader, it will have more than fulfilled its purpose.

3.1. Conversation and Small Talk

I invite the reader to consider the two zones adjacent to the equator, which I called *conversation* and *small talk*. These are the two layers we usually have in mind when we speak of *language*, although we consider them to be one. Of course, they are very broad layers. The conversation layer encompasses processes that range from the conversation between a buyer and a seller on the market up to the progressive conversation that is called *science*. The small talk layer encompasses processes that range from chitchat between two neighbors to that huge chatter that floods us in the form of commercial and political propaganda and pseudo-artistic productions in the cinema, illustrated magazines, and romance novels. Whereas the first is authentic and the other false, they are quite similar allowing to be treated in the same paragraph. These layers consist of networks that can be considered, subjectively, as formed by intellects that irradiate and absorb phrases, and objectively, as formed by phrases that intersect within intellects. In the conversation layer, this process of irradiation, absorption, and crossing is authentic. Phrases are formed; that is, *information* is generated. This information is emitted and becomes *messages*. Intellects are the places within the conversation where information emerges or is accumulated. A new science, cybernetics, studies these processes, without realizing, I believe, the exact territory of its study: the *conversational* layer of language. As a result of this new science, electronic brains are about to participate in this layer of language, becoming, in this sense, something restricted: *intellects*. When Heidegger said that we are *a conversation that began with the*

Greeks, he probably had not foreseen the inclusion of these *new* participants. However, if I read Heidegger correctly, he uses the word *conversation* in a broader sense than the one used here—he uses it in the sense that corresponds to our word *language.* The *electronic* brains will not be *Dasein* (existences) in the Heideggerian sense, even participating, as they likely will fully participate *(horribile visu)* in our conversation. This is because the upper layers of language will be eternally closed off to them.

The constant formation of new phrases, that is, the constant regrouping of words according to the rules of several languages in new formations, and the outbreak of new information always make the territory of conversation constantly grow. In this sense, conversation is productive. It expands the territory of reality and submits to it new regions of relations that were not previously established. The progress of science is the most obvious, and quickest, form of such productivity. In fact, science is conversation in its most perfect and rigorous form. The elements of language are, during this higher type of conversation, constantly regrouped by the participating intellects, in a conscious search for new phrases that obey the rules of the scientific language: mathematics. Participating intellects are not yet fully aware that the elements with which they operate are linguistic and the rules to which they conform are grammatical (i.e., mathematics); they are still likely to naively declare that the elements are *natural* and the rules *natural laws* (without being able to define the word *natural,* of course). Yet the *conversational* aspect of scientific activity becomes ever more evident even to the intellects of its participants. The Newtonian phrase *God is a mathematician* already seems to indicate this direction. Einstein, in many of his paraphilosophical reflections, comes very close to this view of scientific activity. He considers, for example, that the advantage of the modern system of physics over the Newtonian is a *linguistic advantage (vorteilhafte Schilderungsform),* which resides principally in the economy of terms *(Begriffsökonomie).* The famous

Einsteinian aphorism *God does not play dice (Gott würfelt nicht)* acquires, in Portuguese, an even deeper meaning than the intended one. Einstein meant that the *dice (dados),* that is, the playing stones, are not prototypes for the phenomena of nature, because nature obeys preestablished rules. In Portuguese, the second meaning of *dice (dados)* emerges as "data," the raw material of knowledge. I mention this as a curiosity, as an example of a spontaneous irony (perhaps even wisdom?) of language.

The conversational aspect of scientific activity becomes evident in all its branches, as this type of conversation progresses. The naive question, the fruit of a primitive metaphysics, of the type *What is really an atom?* or *What is really a gene?* or *What is really a sublimation?* or *What is really a society?* is the sort of question less frequently formulated by the scientist. I offer two answers to these kinds of questions that demonstrate the awakening of science's self-understanding—Eddington: *Ether is the noun of the verb: to oscillate*; Russell: *The atom is part of matter, just as the M is part of the apple.*

Science is a specially developed and concentrated form of conversation. In it phrases are formulated with the conscious purpose of *discovering* new information; that is, conscious attempts are made to establish new relationships between the elements of language in accordance with the rules. Another type of philosophizing (an inferior type, I believe) is a different form of conversation in this sense. The most conscious representative of this type of philosophizing, it seems to me, is Occam, not only because he is a typical *nominalist* in the medieval sense of the word, that is, by relegating all matters of thought, except *particulars,* to the territory of language, but mainly because of his concept known as *Occam's razor,* according to which the progress of thought lies in the economy of terms. It is curious to see how medieval nominalism approaches a view of language close to the one exposed here, so to speak, on the negative side. Although disregarding language, calling it *flatus vocis,* even nominalism reserves the vast majority of intellectual processes to language. The exception, the proper names, are not considered names, but as signifying extralinguistic realities. This is a small but decisive step that nominalism never gave. From nominalism, in time, the modern scientific mentality emerged. If nominalism had taken that small, decisive step, if the Scholastics had decided on a fundamental ontology of language, if they had actually applied *Occam's razor,* possibly all scientific development would have had a different and more self-conscious effect. We might thus have avoided the false scientism of the eighteenth and nineteenth centuries.

There is, however, another kind of philosophizing that belongs to an upper layer of language because the productivity of the conversational layer is limited. To use the attached graph, I would say that the productivity of the conversation is flat, it develops in two dimensions, it extends language, but it does not deepen it. Conversation is not the creator of new words, of new elements of reality; it is not poetic in the sense of *poēsis,* of *establishing (Herstellen)* reality. True philosophy goes beyond the layer of conversation and participates in the layer of poetry. In this sense, it covers and overcomes science. This is something I will deal with in the next paragraph.

The climate that prevails in the layer of the conversation is of intellects realized through contact with others. The intellects are open to each other; they are real not because they are *here (Dasein)* but because they are *together (Mitsein).* The intellects absorb information emitted by others, that is, they apprehend and comprehend, and they emit new information, that is, they articulate. To speak existentially, the intellects transform the information that is *things* for them into information that will be *instruments* for them; in this productive work, they cease to be determined *(bedingt)* to become free *(bezeugt).* The freedom of the intellect, on the layer of conversation, lies in its transformation of phrases into new information to be transmitted. In this sense, I fear that the electronic brains will also be free. I do not know to what extent the existential thinkers would agree with me in this regard. As can be seen, this is a mechanical type of freedom, the regrouping of fixed and given elements. No wonder the contemplation of this senseless and absurd kind of freedom has caused nausea and despair to honest thinkers like Camus and, to some extent, Sartre. While I believe that all existentialists, in addition to ignoring, at least consciously, the upper layers of language, also underestimate the productive strength of conversation, subconsciously, and almost consciously, all of them operate within the upper layers, and Heidegger almost comes close to formulating an ontology of language. However, fascinated by *nothingness* and without contact with Wittgenstein, he does not come to free himself from the dominance that the German and Greek languages exert upon him.

Even by admitting the productivity of the conversation, and even including all scientific activity (which is not entirely correct, as I will show later), one must painfully admit that the intellect thus realized only *conversing* does not attain full realization. By conversing, the intellect will reside near the equator of our chart, it will be in the center of the fabric of language, and it will not have taken any step to becoming free from language. Socrates, it is true, identifies paradise with conversation. Ever since he took the poison, he has been conversing with his elders in eternity. However, for Socrates, as for Heidegger, *conversation* is a broader term than the one employed here, if we can still grasp some of the spirit of Plato's language. For Socrates to converse *(dialogein)* encompasses a superior creative power, even than that of poetry. But this problem will be dealt with later. Conversation in the narrow sense, as it appears in the graph, is a subaltern form of realization of the intellect. Even so, it is a realization never achieved by many. For most people, the climate is one of small talk.

Viewed superficially, small talk seems identical to conversation. It also consists of nets, apparently formed by phrases and intellects. However, under careful examination, we will see that small talk is composed of conversational debris that penetrates imperceptibly the lower layers, like the detritus of plankton in the sea. The Portuguese idiom *conversa fiada* expresses this situation excellently. Heidegger, who, as I said, comes very close to the formulation of an ontology of language, calls this layer *Gerede*. The German word, however, is inappropriate, and consequently, the Heideggerian concept is also inappropriate. The small talk layer *borrowed* the phrases from the conversation layer. Phrases formulated by intellects participating in the conversation layer are picked up by *pseudo-intellects* participating in the small talk layer, never being fully apprehended or comprehended. I say pseudo-intellects because in this layer, a true intellect does not become realized. They are puppets, imitations of intellects, embryonic intellects, something almost real but still below the equator of reality. From the point of view of the intellects in conversation, these pseudo-intellects are not together *(Mitsein)* but are ready at hand *(vorhanden)* and will be realized only within the intellects in conversation as they are apprehended and comprehended. Thus, viewed from the conversation layer, the networks of small talk are products of the decadence of the conversation networks. They are the almost real specters of authentic conversation; they are frustrated conversations.

The climate within this layer is the closed climate of anguish. The intellects (if they can be called thus) do not absorb the information that falls upon them, apprehending and comprehending nothing. They simply reflect this information mechanically, as if they were billiard balls, and so small talk emerges. Information, *taken* from the conversation, is pushed, undigested, from pseudo-intellect to pseudo-intellect and becomes distorted and misshapen in this process. The pseudo-intellects, closed in on themselves, are a plaything of the information that falls upon them. Entirely encapsulated and surrounded by unapprehended and uncomprehended information, these anguished pseudo-intellects are completely delineated *by things* and have no freedom. For this reason, they are not real in the authentic sense of the word. The electronic brains will be more real than these pseudo-intellects.

This is an infernal image that I have just painted of what, after all, could be a large part of *humanity*. This is the image that we must accept, whether we like it or not, if we are to give credence to the existentialists. Though they may not say so (and do not even know it consciously), this is the image they paint when it becomes exposed in the light of an ontological analysis of language. This image denies the quality of *reality* to a large part of humanity and degrades it to the stage of *thing*, that is, a potential instrument for realized intellects. Could an error be discovered in this argument?

I believe that the error hides again in the simultaneous overvaluation and undervaluation, or rather, in the incomprehension of language by the analyzers. Small talk is a layer of language that can be superimposed on another. The intellect, as it becomes realized in the conversation, is emerging from the lower layers of language. And as it becomes frustrated in its attempt to realize itself in conversation, it falls into the lower strata. *The realized intellect, let us not forget, is the subjective aspect of language.* Like language, the intellect is also a process. Let us visualize this process as follows: intellects who become realized in conversation either project themselves from the conversation layer or tend to fall back into it. As they become realized, they participate in the conversation, that is, they apprehend, comprehend, and articulate. While they are not yet realized, or as long as they are no longer able to realize themselves, they cease to apprehend and comprehend, blindly reflecting phrases, participating in small talk. Therefore, as they become realized, they are free, and as they are still or are no longer realized, they are determined. The intellect, being a process, is only real insofar as it participates in the conversation, and small talk is only the last unreal stage, therefore fictitious, in the realization of the intellect. In our graphic, everything that is below the equator of reality is fictitious in this sense; it is inauthentic language. The limbo of conversation is thus a myth.

However, this myth becomes reality when apprehended and comprehended by the intellect in conversation. The analysis of language, therefore, as it is undertaken here, realizes the myth, not as something existing in a way outside the intellect realized in conversation, and in this lies the error of the existentialists, but as an immediate and ever threatening horizon of the intellect itself. Small talk is not something ontologically independent, some part of humanity that is despicable and usable, but is a very real place, because it is part of the realized intellect, where it can become diluted into nothingness—the place, to speak again as the existentialists do, where the *Self* can dissolve and become *the people (man)*.

The zones of *conversation* and *small talk* are the only ones that have been investigated more or less consciously by existential analysis, and, as I believe I have shown, they were investigated in an unsatisfactory way. It was therefore necessary to clear the field.

In conclusion, I can say this: the intellect, when it becomes realized, does not do so abruptly, emerging from the nothingness of potentiality as Pallas Athena from the head of Zeus. Nor does it emerge irrevocably, as it is always in danger of falling back into the nothingness from which it emerged. It emerges gradually, passing through several zones of a language in statu nascendi. In other words, the intellect is itself the subjective aspect of this language in statu nascendi. As I have endeavored to say in the first chapter, this attempt to describe the origin of the intellect, this attempt, then, to intellectually overcome the intellect, is an analogy, a myth. But at this point in the argument, this attempt is no longer paradoxical. By its own character, the analysis of language allows for it. This analysis uncovers the zone of small talk, as the zone of language immediately prior to the intellect's emergence, and the zone of conversation, within which the intellect begins to become realized. The comparison of the two zones, which language analysis allows for, shows something of the character of the intellect: its productivity when realized in conversation and its unproductiveness when still (or already) in small talk; its freedom when in conversation (somewhat restricted freedom) and its limitation when in small talk; its togetherness with other intellects when realized in conversation and its solipsistic anguish when in small talk. The terrible tautology of language, the repetition of the eternally identical, which terrified Wittgenstein, and which characterizes, from another angle, Nietzschean thought, is the climate of small talk. For Wittgenstein, language is reduced to small talk, and for Nietzsche, the Will to Power (that is, the intellect in statu nascendi) becomes the Will in reaching power, so it never reaches authentic conversation but always falls into small talk. Wittgenstein's despair is the result of his ignorance of the upper layers of language and his consequent overvaluation of small talk. Unaware of conversation, he has to include, for example, science within small talk, hence his rationalist skepticism. Heidegger, in this sense, surpasses both Nietzsche and Wittgenstein and distinguishes the two layers. Yet his ontological analysis is flawed. Not appreciating the mere potentiality of small talk (though calling it inauthentic = not real), he arrives at an unacceptable ethics. From the point of view of this analysis, however, both Wittgensteinian and Nietzschean pessimism as to the epistemological value of language (or life, as Nietzsche would say) and Heidegger's pessimism as to the ethical value of language (or existence, as Heidegger would say) dissipate. However, our optimism is not unlimited. The intellect that is realized in conversation creates reality, but a limited reality, and is always threatened to become annihilated by small talk. The contemplation of other layers of language should shed more light on the process of the realization of the intellect, a realization that was understood as an attempt by the intellect to overcome itself, expanding and finally annihilating itself in the opposite direction toward small talk.

3.2. Poetry and Word Salad

To the north of the *conversation* zone, in the attached graph, I placed an area that I called *poetry*. This name requires a somewhat more detailed explanation. The word comes from the Greek *poietés* (the one who produces something) and *poiein* (to do in the sense of establishing). Its translation into German is *Dichtung* (densification, enclosing, heating). According to the definition of poetry offered by the *Encyclopaedia Britannica,* poetry *is the concrete and artistic expression of the human intellect in emotional and rhythmic language.* In the same article, we find the following line by George Eliot: *Speech is but broken light upon the depth of the unspoken.* Although the writer of the *Encyclopaedia* does not mention this line for this purpose, I believe that it represents a beautiful approximation of a definition of poetry, made by a poet. I shall add my own attempt to define poetry: *it is the effort of the intellect in conversation to create language.* Owing to these considerations, to be clarified later, I decided to give this name to the area under study.

By borrowing a biological concept, I will say that poetry is a mutation of conversation. As in the mutations of biological species, phylogenesis discovers similarities and kinship between conversation and poetry. However, there can be no doubt that poetry is a new kind of language. Plato says that thought is a conversation of the intellect with itself. Because Plato was a poet, we can interpret this pronouncement as a phylogenetic theory of poetry, a theory based on introspection. Plato seems to say that the internalization of conversation results in *thought,* or philosophical thought, which, in Plato's case, is poetry. Let us take this interpretation of the Platonic phrase as the starting point for the investigation of the *poetry* layer, without concern for its *objective validity.*

What is this interiorization of conversation? Conversation has been illustrated as a network composed of intellects that absorb and utter phrases. The interiorization of conversation can be visualized in two ways: as a swelling of the intellect until it encompasses the threads of the network or as a gathering, a shrinking, of the network into the intellect. The German word *Dichtung* suggests the second image. Let us take a closer look at this image, as the German language suggests it. The network of conversation is being gathered, shrunk *(eingeholt)*. It shrinks, becomes dense *(wird dichter)*. The meshes of the net close; it becomes impermeable *(wird dicht)*. The network changed; it became poetry *(Dichtung)*. The fisherman, the intellect, can now repair *(überholen)* the conversation; he can overcome it.

This is the image that the German language offers, according to which poetry is the net of conversation, gathered, shrunk, made impermeable, and overcome by the intellect. The four stages of transformation are important for the understanding of poetry. (1) The gathered conversation means a change of climate. The intellect is no longer together with other intellects but isolated with itself. This is, however, an entirely different type of isolation from the isolation prevailing in small talk. (2) The shrunken conversation means a concentration of language. Its structure becomes denser; new connections between the parties emerge; new rules emerge. As a consequence, the intellect seems to be subject to new limitations; its freedom seems more restricted. This is, however, an entirely different type of restriction from the lack of freedom prevailing in small talk. (3) Once impermeable, conversation means the impenetrability of language by the intellect. Its structure has become dense in such a way that it is impossible to analyze language through the intellect. Every attempt to analyze language at this stage loosens and destroys the quality of impermeability, that is, the poetic quality. The intellect's capacity for apprehension and comprehension seems, therefore, to be diminished. This is, however, an entirely different type of diminution from the prevailing incapacity of the intellect in small talk. (4) Once overcome, conversation means a change in the intellect's position. Instead of being encompassed by language, like a knot in the net, the intellect encompasses language, like a hand holding the shrunken net. Language is in hand *(zuhanden)*; it has become an instrument. In short, I can say that the poet *(Dichter)* gathered the conversation upon himself, that is, he gathered himself, he became concentrated upon himself, imposing himself new limitations; he is in an impenetrable trap, which, when penetrated, dissipates into ordinary conversation and loses its meaning, and he uses such impenetrable language as an instrument.

The word *Dichtung* thus illustrates phylogenesis: the emergence of poetry. The word *poetry* illustrates its functioning. The word *poiein* (to do, to produce) must have a common root with the Latin word *ponere* (to put). The poet is, therefore, a positor, who supplies the raw material for the composers, that is, the intellects in conversation. From the point of view of poetry, conversation is, including the scientific and philosophical kinds already mentioned, a variation on themes proposed by poetry. The poet proposes; the conversation composes. From this point of view, we must say that conversation is the dissipated poetic trappings, therefore, apprehended and comprehended. The activity of the conversation is prosaic (of *prorsus,* "plane"); it is restricted to two dimensions; it spreads reality onto a plane. Poetic activity is productive sensu stricto; it pulls something *(es)* out of the depths of the inarticulate (Eliot: the depth of the unspoken). *To produce* comes from *producere* (to bring to the surface). Poetry is, therefore, the production of language. Whence does the poet produce language? Ex nihilo: from that unutterable nothingness that is the Alpha and the Omega of language.

I ask the reader to refer to the attached graph. Given the position of the area of poetry within the context of language, that is, away from nothingness at both poles, how can poetry go up or down to nothingness to take from it a new language? The ancients knew how: thanks to the Muses. The poets, these mouths of the muses, are the channels through which nothingness spills over language, realizing themselves in it. Poetry is the place where language sucks in potentiality to produce reality. We must therefore imagine our graph as three-dimensional. The globe of language turns in nothingness and is in contact with nothingness on its entire surface. The area of poetic language, being dense and impenetrable horizontally, is therefore opened vertically; it opens like a *mouth*. Nothingness penetrates through this opening, drop by drop, during moments of inspiration, and becomes realized in language. The poet, the open mouth in admiration (Aristotle: *Propter admirationem enim et nunc et primo inceperunt homines philosophari*), is the place where language breathes nothingness in and transforms it into new language. This new language, being incomprehensible because it is too dense, descends into the layer of conversation to become diluted, in order to be apprehended and comprehended. Thus conversation is nothing more than an illuminating, albeit unconscious, critique of poetry.

This is the image that the analysis of the word *poetry* offers. An analysis of the Czech word *básnictví* (poetry) would probably open new vistas onto the same layer of language. However, the vision we have already achieved must suffice for our purpose. Let us try to summarize it: phylogenetically, poetry emerges from the conversation by gathering it, shrinking it, impermeabilizing it, and overcoming it. Functionally, poetry is the creation of new language out of the nothingness that surrounds language on all sides, a language in itself incomprehensible intellectually but made comprehensible after its dilution into conversation. Thus, poetry made more palpable, we can now try to orient ourselves within it.

I will say that the layer of poetry as outlined here encompasses everything that is commonly called *originality*. This word is appropriate, because it indicates that poetry is the place where new phrases have their origin. In German, it would have said that poetry covers the zone of *Einfall* ("incursion," in the sense of original thought). The layer covers, therefore, all authentic poetry *sensu stricto*; it encompasses productive philosophy and embraces those phases of science where new concepts are formulated. It is for this reason that I was reluctant to include all of science in the layer of conversation. In other words, the poet is he who has (and conveys into the conversation) new thoughts. The problem lies in the word *new*. What is this quality of novelty that distinguishes poetic thoughts from prosaic thoughts? It cannot reside in a new recomposition of already existing elements, because this is the normal activity of the conversation. The novelty must lie in the imposition of new rules, according to which elements will henceforth be composed, and in the creation of new elements of language. Thus poetic activity is twofold: it imposes new rules and new words (concepts). Its thoughts (phrases) are new, because they contain new elements (new concepts) or new rules (new grammar). Thus is the famous phrase of Charlemagne to be interpreted: *Ego, Imperator Germanorum, supra grammaticos sto* (I, Emperor of the Germans, am above the grammarians).[1] At this moment, Charlemagne was a poet. In short, poetry is the creation of new concepts (words) and new rules. From this definition, we can arrive at a clearer understanding of freedom. By creating new rules, the freedom of creation (the only authentic freedom), far from being reduced, becomes broader. The new rules make new compositions of elements possible and increase the territory of free choice. Lack of rules, far from representing freedom, represents the chaos of chance, in which all free choice is forbidden by the impossibility

---

1 Flusser rarely checked his sources, so this phrase may not be by Charles the Great but by Emperor Sigismund of Hungary, who was also the Holy Roman Emperor between 1433 and 1437. *Ego Imperator Romanum supra grammaticos sto*. [T.N.]

of predicting the consequences of choice. Therefore the productive activity of poetry, by imposing new rules and new concepts on language, is an activity that creates freedom. The intellects in conversation are progressively freer as they absorb the new rules and concepts imparted to them by poetry.

The isolation in which the poet finds himself is apparently as illusory as his loss of freedom. He is as isolated from the intellects in conversation as are the vanguards of the advancing armies. The poet represents the tip of the wedge that the conversation forces into the unutterable. The poets are our explorers, who expose themselves, for our sake as much as their own, to the danger of annihilation by the unutterable. Far from being isolated, they are, precisely because they have gathered themselves, the conductors of the conversation. The danger of the poet's exposure to the immediate influx of nothingness is constant and imminent. Whereas the danger of the intellect in conversation is falling into small talk, the danger of the poet is the abrupt drop into the word salad so typical of madness.

In his novel *Dr. Faustus,* Thomas Mann introduces a scene (the speech next to the piano) that illustrates this abrupt fall with a stroke of genius. Nietzsche's letters at the beginning of his madness, those which he signed as *Christus Imperator,* are an extreme example of what I have in mind. These examples can be easily multiplied. There is a vast literature on the subject of *genius* and *madness.* I believe the attached graph places this problem within the language set. I put the *word salad* zone south of small talk. I will now try to penetrate this layer of language.

What psychiatry calls *dementia praecox* is, if seen from the perspective of language, the dissolution, and therefore the annihilation, of the knot of the intellect. The threads of phrases (thoughts) that form the intellect when they meet and cross separate themselves suddenly, and the intellect dissolves. Instead of the network of conversation, where the knot was before, suddenly the abyss of nothingness opens up, within which the wrecks of phrases float in an annihilated reality, the word salad. Today, the analyzing intellect, far removed from the origin of language, studies this phenomenon with apparent calm distance. However, when faced with this annihilation of the intellect, witnessing the salad of words as it flows from the mouth of nothingness, or observing the superorganized chaos of the paintings by the demented, we still feel today that *mysterium tremendum* (that mystery that makes us tremble) the ancients felt by regarding madmen as saints. The climate of the word salad zone is the climate of fear, trembling, and teeth grinding. There is a philosopher poet who has voluntarily exposed himself to the immediate influence of nothingness, fully aware that in this exposure lies an authentic, albeit paradoxical, productivity. This philosopher was Kierkegaard. As a result, he always felt immediately threatened by the fall into annihilation, into the word salad. His book *Fear and Trembling* is a vision from the layer of poetry into the layer of this kind of annihilation.

Apparently, there is complete freedom within this zone. Words come together and separate themselves without any apparent rule. But this chaotic freedom is just a sign of the complete impossibility of choice. The Kierkegaardian *aut-aut* cannot function in this dilacerated region of language, where everything is possible and nothing is necessary. The shattered remains of the intellect, wandering and wondering above nothingness, dissolve progressively within it. As the rules disappear, the elements of language also disappear. Language becomes impoverished insofar as it becomes disorganized. There are frantic phrases at this stage, during which fantastic auxiliary structures are constructed and fantastic linguistic elements, caricatures of poetic activity, are invented, which are mirrored in the pseudo-organized writings and paintings of the demented. These phrases are inauthentic, because, instead of emerging out of nothingness, they tend toward it. Although of difficult intellectual analysis, their inauthenticity is felt immediately:

another proof of the impenetrability of poetic quality by the intellect. In sum, the area of the word salad, this area of dilacerated language, is, to a certain extent, a mirror of the poetry zone.

Summarizing what was sketched in this paragraph, I would say the following: the intellect in conversation, in its freedom, limited by the layer in which it finds itself, tends to overcome conversation, by also overcoming itself. It gathers itself, talks to itself (Plato), and turns language into its instrument. Language, thus transformed, allows itself to be overcome by poetry; that is to say, thus shrunken, language leaves an opening within the intellect through which nothingness can become realized. But in this way, language exposes the intellect to nothingness, which, by not bearing this impact, can fall into the madness of the salad of words, which, as the word *dementia* says, is a form of annihilation of the intellect. *Poetry* is anything that brings originality, that is, new thoughts, into the conversation, so this is what we call poetry sensu stricto; this is productive philosophy, and it is the hypothetical phase of science (among other poetic contributions that were not analyzed). However, the intellect in the poetic layer is not fully realized. The intellect is, indeed, exposed to nothingness, and in this sense, it overcomes language. Yet it stands prostrate before nothingness in silent admiration, hoping to be *inspired*. The active search for nothingness by the intellect, its desire for annihilation, will be the object of study in the following paragraph.

3.3. Oration and Babbling

In the attached graph, I called the layer north of poetry *oration*. This word comes from the Latin *os* (mouth) and means, approximately, the *conscious and authentic use of language*. The orator is the one who has apprehended and comprehended the use of language and now uses it. But this word still has a meaning apparently different from the first: it means *to pray* and therefore a conversation with the unutterable. I believe that the two meanings are fundamentally identical: oration is the mouth of language, that is, the extreme articulation through which the unutterable is approached. This oration can take two forms: the forms of peroration and adoration. As seemingly different as they are, I shall attempt to demonstrate that they in fact belong to the same layer. I shall call *peroration* what is generally called *mathematical symbolism* and *logical symbolism,* and I shall call *adoration* all those activities by which the intellect approaches the unutterable.

Oratory, that is, the art of using language, was once a prominent part of the educational curriculum. This is an art that is seemingly falling into disuse. During the eighteenth century, the art of conversation, a kind of subaltern oratory, was cultivated. It too has been relegated to oblivion. Yet this neglect of the art of speaking is only apparent. This is because oratory (the art of conversation) is being replaced by a much more powerful and penetrating instrument for apprehending and comprehending the use of language: mathematical analysis. This analysis, which has its roots already in the Middle Ages, but which really begins to work only two or three generations ago, can be defined as follows: mathematical analysis is the attempt to consciously establish several linguistic layers, *metalanguages,* that are progressively more formal and structural and less meaningful. The last of these layers, that of logical calculus, of algebraic logic, of symbolic logic (or whatever the expression used by its creators), would be purely formal, would encompass all language, and would mean (point to) *nothing.* With this conscious attempt to penetrate and rule language, stripping it of meaning, rendering it tautological and therefore inoperative and harmless, the intellect gathers the layer of *oration* and provocatively faces nothingness.

This analysis proceeds as follows: the phrases of fusional languages (the only ones known by logical mathematicians), which form the conversation, consist of symbols and relations between symbols. The symbols (words) apparently point to something extralinguistic, toward *the reality of raw data*. The relations between symbols are the structure according to which symbols are grouped into phrases. This structure is imposed on them a priori by the intellect. If we could eliminate words (meaningful symbols) and replace them with empty symbols (algebraic signs), and if we could simplify the relations between these empty symbols, reducing them to three or four (the minimum imposed a priori by the intellect), we would have created a pure network of a priori symbols and relations, that is, self-evident. Thus we would have created a universal language layer—automatically comprehensible and free of any possible error. All of its phrases would evidently be correct despite meaning *nothing*. This layer could serve as a frame of reference for all other layers of language. It would only be necessary to translate a sentence from any layer to ours to see if the sentence is correct. However, this layer would allow for a lot more. The observations that the senses make of raw data are necessarily articulated in a lower layer of language, or perhaps they articulate only the relation of negation. These observations could be translated to our layer, compared to other translations, and subjected to the operations of composition and of formal and self-evident recomposition, which are characteristic of our layer. The result could be retranslated to the original lower layer and would result in a meaningful, but evidently correct, phrase.

The epistemological and ontological foundations of this type of language analysis were analyzed and rejected in the first chapter of this work. Therefore only a short reminder of the reason for the refusal is necessary: (1) the structure assumed by logical-mathematical analysis as being common and universal to all languages, therefore a priori in the intellect, belongs, in reality, only to *one* type of language; (2) to say that the symbols of language (words) are signifiers of something extralinguistic is the same as attempting to utter the unutterable—it lacks meaning; (3) by ignoring the diversity of languages, this analysis also ignores the epistemological and ontological problem of translation—it does not know that in the process of translation to, and from, its own layer, meaning becomes distorted and falsified; (4) this analysis confuses the concept, *correct* (in the sense of *in accordance with the rules of language*) with the concept, *true* (in the sense of *in accordance with raw data*). Because this analysis presupposes, however, the reality of raw data, this confusion is unforgivable.

Although logical-mathematical analysis is ontologically unsustainable, as I believe I have shown, it is impossible to deny the enormous attraction it exerts upon the intellect—not only for its theory, which would be conducive to omniscience, but also for its practice, because it appears to work extremely well. The phrases of nuclear physics and astronomy and, to a lesser extent, chemistry and biochemistry can actually be translated with great benefit to the different layers of the mathematical language, where they are subjected to the various operations, retranslated to the respective original layers, and still work. However, even the most ardent supporters of this theory seem to think that phrases from other strata, such as psychology, ethnology, history, refuse to be manipulated in this way. It is true that mathematics strives to adapt to these layers (hitherto unsuccessfully), but this very endeavor has something very problematic and dubious about it.

It seems to me, however, that the explanation of this curious inconsistency between the various layers of language is evident. The layer of nuclear physics and astronomy operates with almost empty symbols in the sense of the theory under consideration. *Neutrons, negative charges, electromagnetic fields,* and so on, are symbols almost as bare in meaning in relation to *raw data* as the symbol x or a or $=$. The translation of physics into mathematics is not, therefore, a very large leap. According to this theory, symbols such as *fear, dance,* and *war* are, however, much fuller. Their translation into mathematics is practically impossible. There is, indeed, the possibility of circumventing the difficulty. We can try a gradual translation. For example, from history, we can translate to economics, from there to physics, and from there to pure mathematics. Or from painting, we can translate to psychology, from there to biology, from there to physics, and from there to pure mathematics. However, thus multiplied, the epistemological dubiety of translation becomes obvious even to the most ardent of believers. It is necessary, therefore, to note something that few people want to accept but that is obvious: the layer of mathematics does not work, either in theory or in practice, for the purpose to which it was originally proposed by logico-mathematicians.

However, mathematics works both theoretically and practically in a completely different sense. It perfectly analyzes the epistemological aspect of languages and proves, theoretically and in practice, that this value is null. By definition, mathematics and symbolic logic are tautological. If we nurture any hope, in the way logical analysts nurture or nurtured, that extralinguistic knowledge is possible logically or mathematically, then this hope is theoretically destroyed by the tautology of mathematics and formal logic. It is practically destroyed by the diminution of *extralinguistic* meaning, insofar as the exact sciences become mathematized. Such theoretical and practical proofs amount to a rational refutation of rationalism.

The modern founder of this school of thought is Frege. He could not have known the desperate result of his enterprise. But his followers, especially Russell and Whitehead, in their *Principia Mathematica,* and Carnap and Schlick, with their neopositivism, must have glimpsed the dead end to which this type of rationalism leads. They did not, however, have the vision, or the courage, to admit it. They expected, as they still do, a miraculous escape. Judging by his famous saying, Carnap predicts this escape in the following direction: *without formal logic, transcendental logic is lame; without transcendental logic, formal logic is blind.* The escape is therefore found in transcendental logic. It is an emergency exit, because it is both extralinguistically and mathematically nonformulable. This is, in other words, an unspoken capitulation.

Wittgenstein is the only one among the mathematical-logical analysts of language to view the consequences honestly. He confesses the tautology of language, confesses the negative value of discursive reason as an instrument of extralinguistic knowledge, sits down, and collapses into deaf and mute mysticism. He gives up peroration to abandon himself to silent adoration.

Several times in the course of this work, I have tried to argue against Wittgensteinian pessimism. Now, it has become clear to me that he can be definitely abandoned. Now Wittgenstein's basic errors clearly emerge. Wittgenstein has a distorted notion of language. On one hand, he does not know how to evaluate the ontological extension of language. He posits the *Sachverhalt* (approximately, "raw data") as something extralinguistic and real and denies the reality of language. It could be said that this is simply an inversion of terms and therefore that his position remains valid. It could be said that what Wittgenstein calls *reality* is called here *the potentiality of nothingness* and what he calls *the emptiness of language* is called here *reality in language*. However, the inversion of terms demonstrates an effective divergence, which becomes evident when we consider the Wittgensteinian position toward language. He is unaware of all the different linguistic aspects, except the formal one. He does not recognize the creative power of conversation and poetry, and he is not aware of the value of the layers that have not yet been presented to the reader. He does not know the existential experience of language. He does not know, therefore, the projection of the intellect toward authenticity within language, just as he does not know the fall toward annihilation. Finally, he does not know of the plurality of languages and of the creative value, although dangerous, that is inherent in translation. It is due to this lack of knowledge that Wittgenstein comes to consider language as being *nothingness*. For him, language is nothing more than what we call *the layer of small talk,* the layer that is translatable to the mathematical layer: *exact small talk*. From this point of view, language is, in fact, *nothing*. And with these considerations, I believe we can abandon Wittgenstein to his fate.

Let us return to the layer of oration under study here. This layer can be climbed, as I have shown, by the logical-mathematical method and will reveal, in this case, nothingness as the ultimate meaning of language. The intellect that follows this method frees itself, in a somewhat strange sense, from the shackles of language, by apprehending and comprehending that language consists only of shackles without something there to be shackled. The intellect comprehends thus that everything obeys the rules of language, that is, that the Self and the Non-Self obey the rules of language, simply because these rules are the creators of the Self and the Non-Self and, therefore, the creators of everything. The climate of this type of language penetration is nausea and boredom. Everything repeats eternally always with the same variations. All sentences are reversible; all are reformulable in a simpler or more complicated form. Apparent progress lies in a reshaping of the eternally identical, of nothingness. The cosmos of logic and mathematics is the cosmos of boredom in gigantic proportions. Language has been thus orated and perorated, and there is nothing left to do but be silent. For such an intellect, if it is honest, it is no longer possible to participate in the conversation, which it interprets as the eternal, inexact, and therefore veiled repetition of nothingness. Such an intellect voluntarily seeks annihilation.

However, the logical-mathematical method is not the only one able to penetrate the layer of conversation. Seen from this layer, the logical method consists of the following: the intellect absorbs the phrases that intersect in it, but instead of reformulating them productively and, thus reassembled, retransmitting them to the fabric of conversation, the intellect digests and restitutes them in their digested form. It then returns to absorb them and restitutes them again, in order to dissolve them progressively. In this way, a vortex emerges around the intellect, into which the fabric of conversation tends to be attracted. The logical-mathematical intellect absorbs the conversation, without contributing anything, and in this way seeks to annihilate it by freeing itself from conversation. This intellect is, therefore, the place where the conversation turns into oration, and by orating until it has been perorated, it dissolves into nothingness. This intellect is a vertical vortex that draws the conversation toward oration, overcoming poetry without ever noticing its consistency. (I ask the reader to consult the graph.) Herein lies its blindness. The logical-mathematical method goes beyond poetry without apprehending or comprehending it. Concentrated as it is on the formal and structural aspect of language, the logical intellect is unable to discover the poetic aspect of language.

The other method of oration, the second art of oratory, consists in concentrating the intellect precisely on the poetic aspect of language and, in contempt of its formal aspect, the logical-mathematical aspect. To understand this method, it will be necessary to return to the layer of poetry and reconsider some of its aspects. The poet, as has been said, is enclosed in the dense and impenetrable fog of language. He is implicated with language. This implication of the intellect with language, this interweaving, this complication of intellect with language, is precisely the characteristic of the poetic situation. When poetry begins to be conversed, the implicit intellect becomes gradually explicit; the complicated situation between intellect and language becomes explicated; the entrapment, the nebulosity, of the situation dissolves; and the poetic situation becomes diluted in the clear and distinct climate of the plain of conversation. The art of oration that we are now considering is the reverse. The intellect starts from the poetic situation, but instead of descending from this situation into the plain of conversation, it intends to continue the ascent toward the peaks of oration, hoping to attain a new clarity. The trappings of poetry are, from this point of view, an intermediate stage of nebulosity between the lower clarity of conversation and the superior clarity of oration. The lower clarity is possible because the plain of conversation is protected against the unutterable by the protective cover of the poetic clouds, which fecundate it with its productive rains. Superior clarity is attained when the intellect penetrates through this protective cover and reaches the peaks of oration, exposed to the immediate radiations of nonlanguage, of enlightened and resplendent silence. In this way, the intellect will have been explicated from the implication with language in a radically different way than from its explication from conversation. The intellect will have left its language behind, will have separated itself from language. While the conversation explicates the language around the intellect, the oration explicates the intellect out of language. Of course, this explication results in the dissolution of language and intellect. The separation between intellect and language, between the subjective and objective aspects of reality, therefore shatters reality. The intellect overcomes language and dissolves. The rest is silence.

The reader will have noticed that, in trying to visualize this situation of oration, I was forced to resort to images that can be considered as mythical. The situation demands it. Myth is defined by Bachofen as *the exegesis of the symbol,* therefore as an explication of meaning. The method of oration is exactly that. The explication of conversation is logical; the explication of oration is mythical. It is therefore inevitable, when it comes to oration, to resort to myth.

At this point in the argument, I must open a parenthesis: there is in our generation a prevention against the mythical way of thinking, a prevention of which I participate in to some extent. This fear of myth, disguised as superiority, is our eighteenth-century heritage, the century par excellence of conversation. Viewed from conversation, regions beyond poetry simply do not exist; they are unreal because they are not conversable. Although language continues to function in them, as I strive to demonstrate, formally and mythically, they are wholly incomprehensible to the intellect in conversation. This intellect is thus led to conclude that, in addition to poetry, language becomes ever more nebulous and confounds myth with babbling, both equally incomprehensible. We will be able to appreciate this confusion a little later on.

However, this prevention against myth is now being overcome, as we are beginning to overcome the legacy of the eighteenth century. Efforts are now being made to explicate myth nonmythically and therefore to penetrate the layer of myth nonmythically. I cite the examples of Bachofen, Jung, and Kerenyi. I believe, however, that these attempts are doomed to failure by the very character of language. If we read these efforts closely, we find that the language of the authors themselves becomes mythical in dealing with myth. The layer of language into which they are entering demands it.

Nonetheless, we must accept the testimonies of the intellects who declare that they have penetrated the region I have called *oration* and who, without exception, describe it mythically. I have in mind above all Plato's myth of the cave and Nietzsche's myth of Zarathustra. I mention these two in particular because both belong to the chain of philosophical tradition accepted by the layer of conversation and because in both (implicitly in Plato, explicitly in Nietzsche) the myth makes palpable the basic identification between mathematics and mythology. Plato and Nietzsche approach the oration zone from two different directions: Nietzsche with the purpose of overthrowing Plato and the *nihilism* that he represents. But the mythical images they offer us are almost identical. I will consider this problem a little later on.

I close the parenthesis and return to the argument. What happens when poetry turns into oration? The comparison with the transformation of conversation into poetry does not serve as a parallel. In the case of this first transformation, we speak of a *mutation,* of an abrupt change of plane. The poet is qualitatively different from the intellect in conversation. Poetry verts,[2] conversation converts. In the case now under study, the transition from poetry to oration is gradual and imperceptible. The poet continues verting, but his verses, instead of being conversed (and therefore basically changed), are now being converted into orations; that is, they continue being verses. The conversion of the verse into oration is imperceptible. The difference may, however, be felt as a change of direction. When poetry speaks toward conversation, the climate differs from that which prevails when it speaks toward oration. In the first case, the poet creates language to enrich it; in the second, he struggles to overcome it, although he continues to create. An example of the first case is Shakespeare, who launches a torrent of new language over the English conversation, transforming it deeply, broadening it, and radically extending it. An example of the second case is Angelus Silesius, whose last verse verted toward conversation is as follows: *Freund, es ist auch genug. Im Fall du mehr willst lesen, So geh und werde selbst die Schrift und selbst das Wesen* (Oh friend, enough now; if you want to continue reading, go and become yourself writing and its essence). These verses, although still directed toward the conversation, already have the quality of oration in the sense of *prayer*.

What is this new quality of the verse that I have called *prayer*? I believe it can be described as a conscious appeal to the unutterable. The poet no longer waits passively for the muse to *inspire* him. He turns now toward *nothingness* and calls it by its name. He prays toward nothingness; he worships it.

---

2   In Portuguese, Flusser uses the verb *verter* from the Latin *vertere*, which means to "turn" or "flip" something. According to the *OED*, the verb *to vert* has the same meaning and etymology and is the root for *invert, convert, pervert*, and so on. Therefore, although it is no longer commonly used, I chose *to vert* in order to maintain Flusser's play on the words *verse, version, conversion, inverted,* and *controverted,* which all share this root. [T.N.]

Let us return for a moment to our discussion of mathematics and symbolic logic. It has become clear, I hope, that the symbols of these disciplines are empty symbols, symbols of nothingness, therefore names of nothingness. Mathematics and symbolic logic therefore call *nothingness,* just as converted poetry calls the same nothingness. Both belong to the same layer of language. I must therefore insert a word of caution. If I have caused in the course of this argument the impression of wanting to accompany the poet on his advance toward *nothingness,* this impression is false. My purpose is to describe language forcibly from within, since I find myself inside it. I have no hope of overcoming language. But I am obliged to include in my description linguistic phenomena that are driven by this hope. I apprehend them; I strive to comprehend and articulate them. I remain, therefore, prey of the conversation layer. For the intellects in oration, my description is, most probably, desperately inappropriate. So be it, for I have never seen the light that illuminates them, neither the cold, penetrating Wittgensteinian one, nor the warm and scorching one of St. Thomas or the Buddha. I feel that the silences within which they plunge are different; I feel I cannot follow the traces they left in the fabric of language. But the difference is inapprehensible and incomprehensible to me. I issued this word of caution because I do not dare to discuss the undiscussable, which is called *faith,* and I wanted to make this very clear.

Let us return to the two testimonies of the layer of language under discussion, which I have mentioned: Plato and Nietzsche. They represent the two extremes of that zone. The Platonic sage, blinded by the light of *ideas* (which, for Plato, is *reality*), returns to the cave unable to continue participating in the conversation. Nietzsche identifies these Platonic ideas with the empty symbols of mathematics and therefore calls Plato and all Western philosophy after him *nihilist.* The Nietzschean sage returns from the plain of conversation to his mountain to contemplate the Will to

Power, which is the eternal recurrence of the same. Viewed from our analysis of language, however, the two sages do the same thing: they overcome conversation and plunge into the silence of peroration or superpoetic adoration of the always identical, always repetitive, always possible, and never reachable. Nietzsche is right when he identifies *Platonic ideas* with the symbols of mathematics and formal logic, and Plato would agree with him to some extent. Heidegger is right when he identifies Nietzsche's *Will to Power* with the same *nothingness* as the Platonic ideas, although, so to speak, as the reverse side of this *nothingness*. The Platonic side of nothingness is reached rationally, logically, and formally; the Nietzschean side of nothingness is reached empirically, pragmatically, and poetically. But it is the same nothingness. The eternal repetition of the always identical proves it. And the mythical language that both use also proves it. From this point of view, we can delineate Western conversation as having two historical horizons: the Platonic and the Nietzschean. At the beginning of each phase, the Platonic sage descends into the cave; at the end of each phase, the Nietzschean sage climbs the mountain. And the conversation continues, weaving its commentary around the eternally recurring.

The region of *oration* is so far from the region of conversation that it hardly seems still to be language. It seems to be the attempt to articulate the inarticulable, to think the unthinkable. There is, however, an area of language, which I called *babbling,* in which the inarticulate and the unthought reign in statu nascendi or in statu moriendi. This is the zone of idiocy. There is a structural parallelism between this zone and that of *oration* to which I want to draw attention before attempting to analyze it. Apparently, language shatters in a parallel form as it approaches both its poles. The zone of babbling is the zone of symbols that symbolize nothing, the area of words without meaning, just like the oration zone. But the emptiness of these symbols is different, because the intention is different. The symbol, as such, intends something. The empty math symbol, for example, intends nothing, points toward nothingness. The idiot's symbol, the babbled word, intends *something*, namely, to become language, but is nothing. The empty symbol of mathematics is real, because it is a language and intends unreality. The babbled symbol is not real—it is a pseudo-symbol; it is not yet, or is no longer, reality. There is no intellect and there are no phrases (thoughts) in this region; there is an amorphous *becoming*, an amalgam of unrealized inauthenticity. German and French existential philosophies call this amorphous stage of the intellect in formation (or decomposition) *man* or *on*, whose very inappropriate translation into Portuguese is *a gente* (people/one/ we/they). What this word wants to capture is the inauthenticity of the French *on dit* (it is said, one says). But because the analysis of language undertaken from this point of view is not profound enough, it does not know how to distinguish between the shallow inauthenticity of the French *on* layer of small talk and the full inauthenticity of the *on* layer of babbling. *People* in small talk are almost *intellect*, and babbling *people* are almost *instinct*. The phrases of *people* in small talk are almost *thoughts*; the words of babbling *people* are almost *raw data*. We are at the point where language falls apart into its raw elements, into the chaos of possibility. It is not surprising, then, that these pseudo-real elements are those that are studied more closely by the sciences of language. We are in the territory of *phonemes, roots of words, the origins of grammar*; in short, we are approaching *original language*, that is, the idiocy of nothingness. Every time the intellect tries to descend to its origins, every time it goes beyond the equator of reality and plunges into the various stages of the emergence of language, it collides against the same barrier; the phenomenon it wants to study disappears into nothingness.

Thus described, the babbling zone demonstrates at one and the same time its similarity to and its difference from the oration zone. Some German existential thinkers, completely possessed by their

language, propose that this similarity and difference be characterized by the contraposition of the words *man* and *es* (untranslatable:
very nearly "it"). However, I believe that this contraposition acquires
a meaning only within the schema of language as it is sketched in
the attached graph, and even so, it will have its falsified meaning
in the translation into Portuguese. The word is already mentioned
in the second chapter of this work. It represents, among other
meanings, the subject hidden in phrases like *it rains (es regnet),
there are people who (es gibt Leute welche),* and *correct (es stimmt).*
The German language allows for structures such as *es denkt in mir*
(it thinks in me), *es bricht aus mir heraus* (it breaks out from me),
es packt mich (it grabs me), *es geschieht mir* (that happens to me).
All these structures provoke in the German intellect an untranslatable climate for Portuguese that can be described as a kind of
confrontation with the unutterable *(es).* For example: *Es packt mich
die Angst* (It grabs me: fear). In this sentence, it is not exactly fear
that grabs me but the unutterable *es,* which then articulates itself
in fear. What the existential thinkers intend is to characterize that
authentic confrontation with the unutterable, which I have called
oration, with *es,* in contrast to the inauthentic confrontation with
the unutterable, which I have called *babbling,* and which characterizes *man.* But they do not even analyze language enough to locate
es within its fabric, nor do they realize that the concept is German
and untranslatable. I introduced the concept in this chapter and in
the graph, along with the concept *man*—despite this analysis being consciously Portuguese—in order to have a foothold for future
translations. (Translations in the sense elaborated in this work.)

   The argument developed in this paragraph is summarized as
follows: the intellect in conversation, feeling limited by language (or
owing to the limitations of conversed language), tends to overcome
itself, transforming into oration. The intellect is able do this in two
ways: by absorbing, devolving, and reabsorbing the same thoughts
(phrases) in the same knot (intellect), until these have become pure

structure, thus linking empty symbols—hence mathematics and symbolic logic emerge—or by converting poetry into an appeal to the unutterable. Thus prayer emerges. In the first case, language becomes a network without knots and dissolves into nothingness. In the second case, the structure of language shrinks to zero and language dissolves into nothingness. Therefore the intellect dissolves together with language. This is a projected, authentic type of dissolution, which the German language characterizes by the word *es*. This is the upper horizon of language. There is also a lower horizon of language, the area scrutinized by science in search of the origin of the language, which I called babbling. This layer has certain structural similarities to the layer of oration and also some deep divergences. It consists of the idiocy of pseudo-words (pseudo-concepts) grouped in pseudo-phrases (pseudo-thoughts) tending to form pseudo-intellects. Its climate is, therefore, one of inauthenticity, of amorphous unreality, which the German language characterizes by the word *man* and the French language by the word *on*. Beyond these two regions, language and the intellect dissolve into the unutterable nothingness that encompasses them. Our discursive observation can follow language, with many difficulties and many deviations (for example, by analogy and myth) to these borderline regions, but there it stops, to return to the layer of conversation. The hope is that the layer of conversation will be somewhat enriched by these excursions toward the north and south poles of language.

3.4. Amplified Language

The *physiology* of language, as it has been developed up to this point, has limited itself to describing the linguistic phenomena sensu stricto. In other words, *language* has been considered a set of visual or auditory symbols called, in the territory of fusional languages, *words*. Of course, we know at this point that these *words* are really elements of phrases (thoughts), realized in intellects, and that being *visual* or *auditory* is a fact secondarily added by the intellect that contemplates them. However, at this point in the argument, we can dismiss a detailed ontological discrimination and use expressions in their broader, more approximate context. I repeat, therefore: we have considered so far only the *physiology* of language sensu stricto. However, we know that the intellect does not think and articulate only these types of symbols, called in our territory *words*. The intellect, therefore, language sensu lato, encompasses a vast region of symbols, which, though similar in their structures (for they also form organizations), have different characteristics. These are secondary words, which are grouped into secondary phrases, and are abstractions or word concretizations (this characterization varies according to the point of view that we assume, as I will show later). I refer, of course, to the vast region of music and the visual arts, and I ask the reader once again to consult the graph.

3.4.1. Music

I will begin my effort to include these regions within the analysis of language, now undertaken, with the consideration of music. I ask the reader to imagine that the axis joining the two poles of the graph is considered as the line between *auditory symbols* (right side) and *visual symbols* (left side). This division is provisional and will be abandoned at the end of this analysis. In this case, the eastern side of the graph drives through spoken language toward music, and the western side of the graph drives through written language toward the visual arts. This division is very crude and will be elaborated in the course of the argument.

The graph assumes that the transition from spoken language toward music occurs along the entire axis of language, therefore on all its layers. The discussion will reveal whether this presupposition is fertile. We begin our analysis at the most *naturally* (i.e., spontaneously) indicated point, from poetry. In the center of this layer, where it is being intersected by the axis, we find, according to our definition of the graph, the poetry that should be both read and spoken. Of course, all the parts of poetry that are generally called *speculative philosophy* or *hypothetical science* will cluster on the left side of the layer and will not enter into discussion in this subparagraph. From the center and tending toward the right side of the layer, poetry, in the common sense of this word, is located, except for *concrete poetry,* which, in this way, is also excluded from this subparagraph. This poetry sensu stricto, although it can be read, wants to be heard. At least this is true in the territory of fusional languages. The character of the writing of these languages alone proves it. The alphabet is basically a musical notation system. Its signs symbolize sounds. Since the Egyptian hieroglyphs were abandoned, fusional languages have no longer succeeded in establishing a pictorial system that is directly a language. Our alphabets are auxiliary systems that represent spoken language. We do not have a written language. Consequently, we are led to believe that this is a universal phenomenon, that spoken language is *original* and that written language emanates from it. When we consider the visual arts, we will see that this is not true. In the territory of isolating languages, the situation is reversed.

If applied to the fusional languages, by not having developed an independent written language, the graph hangs heavily to the right side. Let us analyze the reason for this imbalance. Fusional languages, such as they really are, that is, as sets of thoughts (phrases), function structurally as forms. The relatively stable elements acquire their meaning according to the position they assume within their respective structures. As a result, these languages assume very complicated structures. If it were authentic, written, pictorial language, which is the externalization of the structure of language, like Chinese is, would be, in the case of fusional languages, an unimaginable complication. Therefore it did not develop. In contrast, fusional languages are extremely impoverished of elements.

Spoken language, which is the externalization of these elements as sensation (aesthetically), is, therefore, in the case of fusional languages, infinitely poorer. (Of course, the element of language in this context is not the word but the sensation, the *aistheton* of the word.) The way a word is written or pronounced changes very little of its meaning in the territory of fusional languages, as it is fixed, almost completely, by the position of the word within the phrase. The melody, rhythm, and timbre of fusional languages, although striking, are therefore relatively poor. It was therefore easy to establish a pictorial system that represented this musical poverty, and the alphabet achieves this representation with a few dozen signs, though not always satisfactorily. Thus emerged our written language, which is in reality a secondary spoken language.

Language is, therefore, potentially spoken in the territory of fusional languages. We think a language in order *to be spoken*. The very word *language* attests it. What is the result of this for poetry sensu stricto? Its activity lies, as it was elaborated, in the condensation of language and in the proposition of new structures and new concepts. Poetry sensu stricto is distinguished from productive philosophy and hypothetical science by the type of new structures and concepts it proposes. Poetry proposes innovations of the *aesthetic* type, that is, new experiences. With spoken language being, however, the lived experience of fusional languages, the innovations of poetry sensu stricto tend to be spoken. The poetry of fusional languages tends toward music. *Music is the aesthetic side, the lived experience of fusional languages.*

In this way, we come to formulate a definition of music, which, although incomplete, may serve us for a little longer. Let us now return to the path initially taken from the axis of the graph toward the right. What distinguishes the poetic language sensu stricto from the poetic language of philosophy? By its rhythm, by the melodic value of its vowel elements, by the timbre of its consonant elements, in sum, by musical values. The difference between poetry sensu stricto and philosophy becomes evident when poetry is spoken. And what is the poetic element common to both? The density and originality of language. And what else do they have in common? The kind of structure and symbols, which they also share with the language of conversation. Poetry sensu stricto is a language of the conversation type, but denser, more unique, and which wants to be spoken to provide its musical experience. As we progress to the right side of our chart, this situation changes. Although language density, originality, and musical experience are preserved (or enhanced), the kind of structure and symbols change. The language of poetry, as it moves toward music, replaces *epistemological* and *logical* structures by *aesthetic* structure and substitutes *comprehensible* elements (words, concepts) for *sensible* elements (sounds, pauses). In other words, at the beginning of the movement of language from poetry to music, it wants to be still *true, correct,* and *comprehensible,* but also *beautiful* and *lived.* As the movement progresses, the emphasis is always greater on *aesthetics* and *experience* and less on *logic.* However, given the fundamentally logical and structural quality of fusional languages, it is not possible to disentangle the aesthetic aspect from the logical aspect. On the contrary, as music moves away from language of the conversation type, to the extent, therefore, that *comprehensible* symbols are replaced by *sensible* symbols, the logical quality of language stands out along with aesthetics. At the end of this process, in the upper layers, as I shall yet show, the two merge.

By now we know enough about music to understand that our point of departure in poetry was entirely arbitrary. This choice owes from the start to the common concept that both *poetry* and *music* are *arts.* Within our system of language analysis, the word *art* is superfluous and can be abandoned (by the Occam's razor principle). Fusional languages tend, in all layers, to the side of music. When moving from the verbal type to the musical type, all the layers retain their characteristics, as analyzed in the previous paragraphs. Thus the layer of conversation corresponds to a layer of music that composes and recomposes elements and structures that are proposed to it by another layer of music that corresponds to poetry. The intellect implicated in this poetic layer of music grabs and pulls out its structures and concepts from nothingness; this intellect is a *poietés*.

However, it is worth taking a moment upon the *oration* layer of music. We find that there is a rather accidental resemblance between mathematics and music. This resemblance is typical of fusional languages; however, the ancients thought this was a universal and characteristic resemblance natural to the universe. They could not have thought otherwise; they only knew of fusional languages. Insofar as musical language reaches the layer of *oration*—that is, insofar as it wants to overcome itself consciously, becoming empty and calling to *nothingness*—its structure becomes evident, which is the structure of fusional languages, therefore purely symbolic and logical. But curiously, its aesthetic quality intensifies to the same extent. The more logical the music, the more rigorous it is; the less meaningful, that is, thematic, the more beautiful it is. And now, seen from the perspective of music, suddenly the aesthetic quality of mathematics emerges. The boredom of the always identical in mathematics, the nausea of the always recurrent in its reversible phrases, disappears as if by charm. In these rarefied layers, where language dissolves into the unutterable, distinctions disappear; math, prayer, and music confuse themselves in a single whole that is about to be annihilated. This aesthetic quality (why not say it?), this musical quality of mathematics, is, most likely, the real attraction it exerts upon the intellects. Conversely, the mathematical quality of music in the layer of oration makes music the major contribution from fusional languages to the totality of conversations that make up reality.

In the inauthentic layers of language, we can observe the same process of transition from conversation-type language toward music-type language. The layer of small talk corresponds to the pseudo-music of *kitsch* and the sentimentality of *the people*. They are debris of music, without message and without information, which are neither apprehended nor comprehended by the pseudo-intellects who participate in this layer. To the layer of the salad of words corresponds a layer of pseudo-music, which consists of screams and noises, so well known in asylums, or in superorganized and inauthentic sonorous systems, that manifest madness. In the layer of babbling, just as in the layer of oration, the two languages merge. At this idiotic level reside the elements of music, just as verbal language does, and they are fundamentally the same. Music shatters and melts in the growling and grunting of inarticulate raw data.

But where does music end up on our chart? What will happen if we persist in our advance from verbal language to the east? I propose that the answer to this question be moved to after the second part of this paragraph. From now on, I can insinuate that it will not be in this horizontal direction that we can overcome language.

3.4.2. Visual Arts

If we consider the left side of the graph, the one in which language slides from written language toward visual language, we will find, in the case of fusional languages, a certain difficulty in establishing a continuity of tendency. For example, there seems to be a deep chasm between verbal language and a statue, in effect, an ontological abyss. Whereas conversation is, according to this analysis, realized potentiality, the statue seems to be something extralinguistic, therefore unreal, although of a dubious ontological position. After all, it is difficult to say that the statue is not *realized,* because it is evidence of the productive work of the intellect. This consideration undermines the whole concept of *reality,* as it is being elaborated here. However, this doubt is clarified if, instead of considering fusional languages, we try to analyze, even from the outside, the isolating languages, the other civilizing conversation.

In the first chapter of this work, which I called the *morphology of language,* I tried to cast a glance at this territory, which is so difficult to reach and so fascinating. Isolating languages are the only partner, and therefore the only system of comparison to ours. Keeping in mind all the difficulties mentioned therein, I venture again on an expedition to the isolating regions. In our languages, the thoughts that form into structures called *phrases* appear in the isolating regions as groups of elements isolated from each other, which I called (borrowing a plastic image) *mosaics.* Isolating languages consist of very few elements, a few hundred *syllables,* which cannot be considered equivalent to our words. A word is an organ of a thought; therefore it has a predetermined function. An isolated syllable, however, only acquires the character of *element of thought* within a set. I will try to illustrate this difference. The fusional word is like a clockwork wheel. It works only inside the watch and will work according to the place reserved for it inside the clock structure. Outside the clock, it does not work, although it *has meaning,* so we know roughly how it will work. The isolating syllable is like a piece of a *jigsaw puzzle.* We know that it is part of the game and that it will work inside within it when put in its place next to the other pieces, but we do not know, if considering it in isolation, how it will work outside of the game; it *has no meaning* on its own. The illustration is not perfect. The word is more flexible than a clockwork wheel, and the isolating syllable is more versatile than a jigsaw puzzle piece. However, I hope this clarifies the difference.

Given this basic character of isolating languages, namely, the lack of structure and the poverty and versatility of its elements, the question arises, What completes thought? How is such an enormous wealth of thoughts as that confronting us in the isolating conversation possible, with so few elements grouped without structure? The answer is not entirely understandable to the logical spirit of fusional languages but points to the music region of our languages. Isolating thought is meaningful in a sense similar to the meaning of our music, therefore aesthetically. The meaning of isolating thoughts is an aesthetic aura around its elements. The isolating languages are musical. Their meaning depends on their musicality.

The consequence of this circumstance is the great difficulty of isolating languages to be spoken. Every inflection of tone, every change of rhythm, every increase of voice changes the meaning. Those who speak isolating languages are understood with difficulty. We have a slight illustration of this in the field of our languages. English is the language that most closely approximates the isolating type. The frequency of the request for spelling is known during the English conversation. In contrast, isolating languages, having few formal elements and no structure, ask to be expressed pictorially. A written language springs organically from them. As a result, the isolating intellect thinks pictorially, thinks in ideograms, almost as exclusively as we think through spoken language. But there is one basic difference, in that the isolating intellect has two distinct possibilities of articulation: speaking and writing. These two possibilities are independent of each other. The isolating intellect can (or is obliged to) speak one thought and write another thought. The translation from spoken language into written language, and vice versa, requires an effort of translation, as analyzed in this work. Our intellect has only one means of expression: spoken language. Our written language is secondary; it is an annotation of spoken language, and there is an almost perfect point-to-point correspondence between the two. Our translation effort is practically nil.

The illiterate in the territory of isolating languages is an intellect not entirely realized. He or she lacks a whole dimension of expression. This is a truncated intellect. As our chart was made from the fusional point of view, it does not contain the layer within which such an intellect should be located. Authentic isolating conversation develops in two dimensions: spoken and written. And there is more. The confusion of languages in the fusional territory is paralleled in the isolating territory only with regard to spoken language. Written language is universal in the territory of isolating languages. What mathematics and symbolic logic want to be in our territory, their written language is authentically within the territory of isolating languages. Our conversations are manifold on all layers, except perhaps in the layer of oration and babbling. The isolating conversation is unison on all layers.

Let us consult our chart and begin the journey from the axis again westward from the layer of poetry, keeping in mind what has just been said. The intellect implicated in the layer of isolating poetry cannot be a philosopher or scientist in the sense in which we understand these words. It cannot take from nothingness new structures or concepts, because for isolating languages, there are no structures or concepts in our sense of these terms. What their intellect proposes, what it verts toward the layer of conversation, are new ideograms. Poetry in this territory wants to be seen, and read.

What is an ideogram? It is a set of pictorial signs (brushstrokes) that corresponds, vaguely, to a concept. The difference is that the ideogram is composed of other ideograms; it is, therefore, a concept containing concepts. The ideogram itself is already a mosaic. The poet, in composing ideograms, is a composer in the true sense of that word. But by creating, proposing new concepts, he is also a philosopher and a scientist. As it turns out, our classifications do not apply to the territory of isolating languages. However, the poetic quality of the ideogram lies not only in its design but also in the way it is drawn. The poetic quality is also calligraphic. There is, therefore, no delineation between *poetry* and calligraphy, between *philosophy* and calligraphy, or between *science* and calligraphy. Isolating poetry is located to the left of the axis on our graph and tends to move toward the visual more radically than our poetry sensu stricto tends to move toward music. *The visual experience is the lived experience (the aistheton) of isolating languages.*

As language shifts from the verbal type to the visual type, the calligraphic quality increases in intensity and the ideographic quality disappears. Nevertheless, it conserves something of the ideographic to the end. The drawings, paintings, statues, pavilions, temples, weapons, instruments, and objects of daily use are progressively *sensualized,* always moving away from verbal language. However, they always retain something of the ideographic, something of the quality of the language from which they emerged. Chinese dragons, Japanese kimonos, Khmer lacquer boxes, are, in essence, colorful ideograms.

Let us try to keep up with this development in the various layers of language. What we can call *drawing and painting* sensu stricto corresponds to the layer of poetry. This is the layer where they emerge, where they are pulled out of nothingness, and where new forms and new auras of meaning are proposed and produced. What we can call *technique and production of implements* corresponds to the layer of the conversation. The forms proposed by poetry are poured onto this layer and are transformed into what we call *material civilization.* The productivity of conversation consists in applying these forms to ever more instruments. The intellect in conversation becomes realized by producing *material civilization*— by converting the forms verted upon it by poetry. The painter-poet's conscious attempt to overcome himself, to abandon his language and to appeal to *nothingness,* corresponds to the layer of oration. Nothingness penetrates the brushstrokes; the silk roll becomes ever more empty and less meaningful; isolated brushstrokes, sometimes soft, sometimes brutal, float on the virgin silk, eventually becoming lost and falling quiet. The rest is silence.

I believe that I can be excused from the effort of following the same sliding of language toward visuality in those layers of language below the equator of reality, which I have called *inauthentic.* Its development parallels that of music in the territory of fusional languages. The problem that now arises is to locate the activities mentioned earlier, namely, painting and sculpture—the material and visual civilization of oration, within the fabric of fusional language. As I have said, at first glance, all these activities seem to be extralinguistic and ontologically different from language, when viewed exclusively from the point of view of our languages. However, today, there is an awakening of intellects in relation to the real situation and therefore in relation to language. I am referring to the emergence of the so-called *abstract and concrete painting* and the so-called *concrete poetry*. I believe that this is an authentic revolution in the territory of our languages, namely, the first almost conscious attempt by fusional intellects (since the age of the Egyptian hieroglyphs) to create a fusional pictorial language independent of spoken language.

If I interpret this development correctly, then the poetic layer of conversational language in our languages corresponds to an incipient pictorial layer that is formed in the following way: fusional poetry sensu stricto, that which is located in the center of its layer and tends toward the right, emphasizes the musical elements of language, while retaining the structural elements. So-called *concrete* poetry emphasizes the structural elements and progressively neglects the musical elements. But that's not all. Concrete poetry uses our alphabet for purposes not originally intended, namely, to be an immediate expression of thoughts, not as transcription of spoken thoughts. It uses the alphabet almost pictorially, not to say ideographically. *O*, for example, is no longer used as representing a sound that is the element of a word, which in turn is a concept. But the *O* directly expresses a concept, to be translated later to spoken language as *circularity, wholeness, closedness,* or *security.* This *O* thus becomes a quasi-ideographic element of a new incipient language within the territory of our languages: the independent, written fusional language. Concrete poetry wants to be seen, not spoken. It is therefore located to the left of the axis on the graph.

As language moves in that direction, the conversational elements of language are being abandoned and the pictorial elements are being emphasized. What remains are structural compositions of lines, planes, bodies, and colors. *Abstract* painting and sculpture emerge.

It is instructive to compare this *concrete* poetry and this *abstract* painting with the poetry and the painting of isolating languages. The difference is revealing. While isolating poetry and painting reveal to the end the antistructural and fundamentally *aesthetic* character (of the lived experience) of their language, our concrete poetry and abstract painting inadvertently reveal the structural and logical, if not mathematical, character of our languages. Abstract paintings are close to geometric constructions; our abstract statues are close to models of non-Euclidean spaces. This, in itself, is a sign of their authenticity. They are authentic expressions of language, just as music is on the other side, which also reveals its kinship with pure logic and mathematics.

If this analysis of language is correct, we are forced to say that what is usually called *figurative* or classical painting and sculpture does not participate in the layer of poetry. Rather, it participates in the layer of conversation. It is part of *material civilization,* such as architecture, everyday instruments, and implements. But how did this form of activity come about, since until very recently, there was no authentic poetic layer to propose forms? How could fusional intellects converse *sensorially*; how could they compose instruments, if there were no poets to propose the theme? The answer, it seems to me, is this: in the territory of fusional languages, there was, indeed, no pictorial language, an independent written language. However, fusional thought has always been potentiality expressible pictorially, and this pictorial aspect of language is called *style*. We can visualize the situation as follows: on the left side of poetry, there were, until very recently, no intellects implicated in poetic language; there were no knots of poetic thoughts. But there were loose thoughts. The pictorial *aesthetic* poetic language was not subjectively experienced as intellects, but it was objectively experienced as a set of thoughts, as a *style,* as what the Germans call *Zeitgeist.* That style, that *Zeitgeist,* is what objectively grasped and still grasps structures and concepts from nothingness to vert them into conversation. *The nonintellectualized style is the poet of our visual activities.*

I believe that the layer of visual oration is underdeveloped in the territory of our languages. There are moments, in the history of our conversation, when the intellects come close to it. I think, for example, of the golden background of Romanesque paintings and Byzantine icons. I think of the columns and the windows of Gothic cathedrals. I think of the arabesques of Islamic illumination and architecture. In the latter case, it seems to be a conscious use of the Arabic alphabet to overcome language in a quasi-ideographic sense. There is, on the other hand, classical Greek architecture, which comes close to the pure structure of logic and mathematics and becomes empty in this sense. But, viewed as a whole, fusional language has not been fertile in its appeals to *nothingness* through visual forms. Perhaps this is a challenge for the future.

There is, however, a development of paramount importance within the fusional conversation, which requires a separate study. I must limit myself in this work to a simple sketch of this problem. This is the result of the poetic activity that I called *hypothetical science* and that tends, in our chart, toward the visual side of language. This poetic activity is relatively new and calls for an ontological analysis from the point of view of language. Heidegger, who so rigorously distinguishes *Ding* (thing) from *Zeug* (instrument), is unable, owing to his basic blindness as to language, to distinguish between the instrument produced by imposition from poetry sensu stricto and the instrument produced by imposition from *scientific poetry.* He does not distinguish ontologically between *portrait* and *machine,* between *horse* and *airplane,* between a *handmade vessel* and an *industrially manufactured vessel.* Our generation is being brutally confronted by these two types of conversation, and we are forced to choose between participating in one or the other. The technical conversation (in the modern sense of the word) threatens to supplant the poetic conversation sensu stricto, at least in the visual part of language. It is imperative that we try to ontologically apprehend and comprehend this process.

What I called *hypothetical science poetry* is located on the left side of the poetry layer. The intellect implicated in this layer pulls from nothingness new structures and new concepts of a special kind, to incorporate them into language. These structures and concepts are called *scientific hypotheses* and refer to the visual activity of language. Obviously, they obey the general character of our languages; they are logical and reducible to pure mathematics. These new concepts and new structures are proposed by scientific poetry to scientific conversation, in order to be conversed. But scientific conversation itself tends toward the visual side of language. In this displacement, scientific conversation progressively replaces the verbal elements of language by pictorial elements, and thus machines and their products emerge. But the analysis cannot stop there. In discussing the layer of conversation, we find that a science called cybernetics naturally took the conversation itself as its theme, as an imposition from scientific poetry. As a result, we will soon witness the visual products of this conversation about conversation, namely, electronic brains participating in the wider conversation as if they were intellects. The same is happening on the left side of the layer. The products of scientific conversation on the visual side, automated machines, will soon participate in the productive activity of this layer as if they were intellects. The ontological appreciation of this new development of fusional languages is a task for the future. We can, however, venture two poetic hypotheses. (1) This new type of intellect will replace the present type by moving it into the small talk layer: in this hypothesis, *humanity* will become *the people*, as an inauthentic and unrealized form. Or (2) this new type of intellect will replace the current type, shifting it toward the layer of poetry: in this hypothesis, what we call *humanity* will be realized more fully thanks to the new type of intellect produced by it. I regret that the scope of this work does not allow an analysis of this problem, but I hope to have at least located it in its context.

Summarizing what was said in this paragraph, I can formulate the following: language, as this concept is used in this work, is broader than the restricted use of the word implies. It covers all forms of thought and all activities of the intellect. Of course, language in the strict sense is the prototype and the cradle of other forms of language that extend to the right and left of the graph. These extensions of language I have called *music* and *visual art,* and together they form the whole of *language,* that is, of *civilization,* that is, of *reality.* This analysis allowed the location of music within the fabric of fusional languages, of painting within the fabric of isolating languages, and of all the activities of so-called *material civilization,* including modern technics, within the fabric of fusional languages. It remains to consider, to conclude this attempt of a *physiology* of language, the reverse side of the globe, as proposed in the attached graph.

3.5. Civilization

What happens when we follow language as it moves toward music or visual art, without ever stopping? Undoubtedly, this pursuit of language in the horizontal sense requires a mental and imaginative effort, because at a given moment, we will no longer find intellect. If, for example, we pursue language in the layer of poetry toward music, we find the following phenomena (enumerated in a very summary way): epic poetry, lyric poetry, song, song without words, instrumentally executed sonata, and perhaps, finally, a type of composition that, in order to be appreciated, does not need to be executed. It can be appreciated as it was proposed by the poet; in musical notes, it can be read. Let us enumerate in the same summary way the phenomena that we will encounter when pursuing language in the layer of poetry toward visual art: sonnet, concrete poetry, *concrete* painting, *abstract* painting, and, possibly, painting so abstract that it does not have to be executed. It can be appreciated as proposed by the poet, as annotations of analytical geometry; it can be read. However, we can take a step further in both directions. Music, as radically musicalized as it was in our last example, may be notated, not in musical symbols, but in more abstract symbols (wave frequencies, decibel volume, rhythm in seconds). Painting, as radically pictorialized as it was in our last example, may be notated, not in geometric symbols, but in pure point coordinates. These coordinates will, of course, correspond to a *time* coordinate. In this way, by radicalizing music, we will be *spatializing* it, and by radicalizing painting, we will be *temporalizing* it. In other words, music will be language stopped in space, and painting will be language stopped in time. Or music will be temporalized painting and painting will be spatialized music. Together, music and painting will become language as a whole, in all *four dimensions,* to speak pseudo-scientifically.

Let us return, for a moment, to the second chapter of this work. The purpose of the argument developed there was to demonstrate how the so-called *categories of reality and knowledge* are, in effect, language categories that vary from language to language. In principle, space and time are, in fact, categories of all fusional languages, although they probably are not to all languages (which is something we can apprehend but not comprehend). However, *space* and *time* do vary from language to language and can be unified in the field of fusional languages, but only through a translation effort, which falsifies them. What I have just said about the problem of music and painting was done from the point of view of the Portuguese language. This consideration merits analysis. What happened in the course of the argument?

I set off from the poetry layer of language. However, if I had wanted to speak with rigor, I should have said that I started from the poetry layer of the Portuguese language. It is true that I formulated this layer in one of the preceding paragraphs, having resorted to German, Greek, and Latin, to arrive at a formulation that is approximately valid for at least similar fusional languages. However, this effort has only relative value. Now, by radicalizing the layer, extending it in both directions, this circumstance becomes evident. Music and painting truly merge, are truly the verse and obverse of the same set: they are, in effect, the poetic layer of the language in which they are being apprehended and comprehended, or in which they are being produced, in this case, of the Portuguese language. Moreover, at the meeting point between music and painting, that is, in the antipodes of the Portuguese language, this becomes evident; the typical structure of that language reappears with its time and space. In other words, and to generalize: when we radicalize language in both directions, when we move away in both directions from the central axis of language, we end up returning to this axis. The extension of language in the horizontal sense does not therefore pass from an extension of its exteriorization; it does not affect the nucleus of language.

It is for this reason that I stressed at the beginning of the previous paragraph that the division of symbols into *visual* and *auditory* is a provisional division and does not fundamentally affect the discussion. The fact that the symbol is *auditory* or *visual* is external to language, and as was said in the first chapter, the symbol is what the intellect expels, expresses, expulses, finally, articulates, toward the senses. Therefore the whole language set that has been studied in this chapter, that is, all the externalizations of language in all its layers and all its extensions, are expressions, articulations of language, and therefore, to a certain extent, excrements of language. They are products of the intellects in conversation and in this sense have already been eliminated from it. To be more exact, all externalized languages, all products of the activity of the intellect in conversation, are the ashes of this activity, in sum, *civilization*. They are ashes that mirror this activity and whose contemplation illustrates this activity, but they are not part of it. *Externalized language, that is, civilization (including material civilization), is an outdated reality.*

This is, of course, a horizon of language that appears for the first time in the course of this work. Language, in its advance from potential toward potential, takes place and leaves behind, as ashes, civilization, that is, a separate reality. This horizon of language could not be introduced earlier because it could have given rise to misunderstandings. It was first necessary to define *civilization as the set of articulated conversation*; it was necessary to illustrate how this articulated conversation closes itself in music and painting, circling, eventually returning to nonarticulated conversation.

From this vision of reality, we can arrive at an understanding of *concrete* and *abstract* concepts, concepts that are basic to the structure of our languages. Concrete language is language in articulation; it is the language that constitutes and unites the intellects. The further it expresses from this process, the more abstract it becomes—abstracted from reality. Abstraction is, therefore, an effort by the intellect to overcome language in the horizontal sense. In this sense, material civilization is more abstract than verbal conversation sensu stricto and represents a greater effort by the intellect to overcome language. All civilization, therefore, and especially material civilization, is the result of an effort of abstraction by intellects in conversation, in order to overcome themselves, by overcoming language. This is an intellectual effort to disintegrate themselves. In other words, language, when realized, superrealizes itself, leaving behind the abstractions of this superrealization, namely, civilization. Language proper, the nucleus of language, is only the axis of our graph, along which language projects itself.

I shall summarize what has been said in this chapter as follows: the *physiology of language*, that is, the study of linguistic processes, reveals that language consists of several layers of realization, or authenticity. Language emerges from the unreachable potential and condenses through the layers of babbling, word salad, and small talk until it becomes realized, that is, until it forms the intellects that apprehend, comprehend, and articulate within the layer of conversation. The process of continuous condensation beyond this layer passes through the layer of poetry to the layer of oration, where it consciously dissolves into the unreachable potential. This process is reversible. Language decays along the same axis from which it projects itself, therefore annihilating itself. In the course of projection, language articulates itself, producing civilization, which means potentiality realized and overcome by reality. As language is projected, the layer of poetry, which pulls new language from the potential that envelops it, enriches it. This is, therefore, the real situation, if this analysis offers a sustainable vision: the activity of realization called language, composed of the intellects in conversation, projects itself from nothingness to nothingness, always in danger of falling into nothingness; however, in projecting itself, language realizes itself in an ever richer and fuller way. This army of intellects in conversation, whose pioneers are the poets and whose outposts are the masters of oration, extends the territory of reality in every direction, conquering it from nothingness. However, these intellects feel that to be fully realized, they must overcome themselves by voluntarily annihilating themselves. The most advanced among them tell us that we are still conversing, and they do it through myths, as in the regions where language dissolves into the unutterable. These myths, in the form of adorations, or in the form of pure mathematics, or pure music, or pure painting, are the utmost expression of language. They are the highest point we can still glimpse, albeit inaccurately. The rest is lost in the quietness of the unutterable *silence*.

4

Language Propagates Reality

4.1. History, Nature, Civilization

The great conversation that we are and that began, if historically seen, with babbling, the word salad of thoughts, and the intellects that have been projected toward realization for thousands, or perhaps tens of thousands, of years, continues its advance toward the unutterable on an increasingly wider front. Thanks to this advance, the territory of reality has expanded and deepened in a way that must seem miraculous, if considered in its historical perspective. The beginning of conversation, the part that began to condense south of the equator of reality, is impenetrable to our intellects. The ashes that this pseudo-conversation left behind, the half-articulated civilization of implements called *eoliths* that stand halfway between *raw data* and *instruments,* testify to the half-conscious attempt by the forming thoughts, by the intellects in statu nascendi, to become realized. If we want to glimpse the nebulous and diffuse world of this incipient conversation, which has developed, all of it, within the layers of babbling and word salad, we must imagine the atmosphere of the unreal, of the dream, of the idiotic unconsciousness, and of the terror of madness. Nebulous thoughts wandered in nothingness, searching for an intellect to articulate them; forming intellects wandered through the terrifying nothingness in search of thoughts to apprehend and comprehend terror and destroy it. In this unreal climate, the fabric of language was formed. However, the historical aspect should not obscure the fact that this stage of language is not overcome. So-called *depth psychology,* which is in reality a kind of unconscious analysis of the lower layers of language, has discovered the immediate presence of this stage of language, apparently historically overcome, and in this discovery resides this field's greatest merit. We, the intellects who have historically formed the most advanced surface of language today, are always threatened individually and collectively with decay into the *man* of babbling and the salad of words. The fabric of language is a fragile structure constantly threatened with annihilation by the nothingness that surrounds it on all sides. This is a precious heritage that has been left to us by our ancestors, to be preserved and increased; otherwise, we will be annihilated. If it were not for the intimate closeness of language to our intellect, if we had the possibility to contemplate it from a distance, our admiration for language would be uncontained. This language, which we are, as it has poured toward us to form us, is the accumulation of all wisdom, of all creative effort, of all the victories, and of all the defeats of the intellects that preceded us. All our thoughts, of which we are composed, carry the mark of our predecessors, both in their concepts (words) and in their structure. Every word, every grammatical form, is a message that reaches us from the bottom of the well of history, and history speaks to us through every word and every grammatical form. The search for the archaeological and historical remains of a civilization in the ashes that the historical disciplines are undertaking is incomparably less significant than would be a historical study of the words and grammatical forms and rules within our intellect. Each of us, being an intellect, is therefore a living formation of history and archaeology. It is this aspect of our intellect that Dilthey glimpsed in attempting to establish his *Geisteswissenschaften* (sciences of the spirit) and by striving for a *comprehensive psychology (verstehende Psychologie)*. This is an authentic, poetic vision that Dilthey has verted toward the conversation; however, I believe it becomes comprehensible only within the general scheme of language appreciation.

The opposition of the *natural sciences* to the *sciences of the spirit*, formulated for the first time by Dilthey, can be located, ontologically, within our appreciation of language. The sciences of the spirit, which, incidentally, have not yet been rigorously formulated, will be a study of language from the historical point of view as outlined earlier and probably executed by the phenomenological method of Husserl. Nothing of these sciences will have anything psychological, and here lies Dilthey's error. The intellectual phenomena, interpreted by the sciences of *the spirit*, will be linguistic phenomena and have nothing to do with psychology. Psychology will continue to be a *natural* science, and so it will belong to another field of research. Husserl, in his struggle against the psychologization of the intellect, comes very close to the identification of intellect with language. In his *Logische Untersuchungen*, he hesitates to formulate concepts that seem to provoke this identification. When, for example, he speaks of the *intentionality of consciousness*, in the sense that consciousness *intends*, that is, *tends* toward something, he comes very close to the symbolic aspect of language. This Husserlian *intentionality of consciousness* is precisely the symbolic meaning of language that is realized as intellect. When Husserl establishes, in *Untersuchungen zur Phänomenologie und Theorie der Erkenntnis*, the priority of pure logic and intends to *take logical ideas, i.e., concepts and phrases, up to epistemological clarity and distinction*, he is almost consciously researching the structures of fusional languages as the foundation of knowledge. The *sciences of the spirit* will therefore be disciplines that dialectically surpass the visions of Dilthey and Husserl and will investigate reality *objectively* (to speak with Husserl) by researching the intellect as a product of the historical development of language. This research will have reality as a whole as its field of activity, since the intellects in conversation are reality as a whole. In sum, the *sciences of the spirit* will be the research of conversation in historical depth.

What are, as opposed to this definition, the *natural* sciences? What is this *nature* that they research? To understand the ontological aspect of this question, let us return to the language stage that I have tried to evoke as historically primitive. What was nature at this unreal stage of babbling and the salad of words? The answer is simple, though it may seem at first glance paradoxical: there was no nature. What we call natural phenomena—stones, stars, rain, trees, hunger—are real phenomena, because they are concepts, words. The relationships between phenomena are real because they form thoughts, phrases. At the stage of babbling, there were no real phenomena of nature; there was only a nebulous chaos of concepts and phrases in formation; there was nature in statu nascendi. As conversation formed, nature emerged. *Therefore nature is a consequence of conversation.*

As conversation progresses, nature is transformed. The *physis* nature of the Greeks is something entirely different from the nature of the current conversation. It is not only the relations between phenomena that are different. See the famous phrase by Anaximander: *the nonlimited is the original material of existing things. Furthermore, the source from which existing things derive their existence is also that to which they return at their destruction, according to necessity; for they give justice and make reparation to one another for their injustice, according to the arrangement of time.* This phrase reveals a relation between the phenomena of *physis,* which lacks meaning within the scheme of our nature and is certainly distorted by translation until it becomes almost incomprehensible. Not only are relationships different but concepts are also different and much more numerous with the development of conversation; the phenomena of nature develop and increase in number as the conversation progresses. The stone of the Greeks, that heavy and dead phenomenon, a by-product of the life of the cosmos that seeks its rightful place by falling, is a phenomenon different from our stone, which is an electromagnetic and gravitational field whose behavior is predictable only statistically. Electric charge, X-rays, chemical reaction, biological heredity, and Rh factor are natural phenomena not realized by Greek conversation, as they were not part of *physis*. They are products of a later conversation to the Greeks.

The following problem arises: if *nature* is a consequence of conversation, as is *civilization,* how are they distinguished from one another, because they are apparently contrary concepts? The answer is this: *nature* is a product of the conversation ontologically prior to *civilization*. Before producing *civilization,* conversation produces *nature*. Nature emerges in the course of conversation, at the moment of the formulation of concepts and phrases. Civilization emerges when the formulation of concepts is already accomplished. In this sense, we can say that nature is the condition of civilization and that civilization is nature transformed.

Civilization has the mark of the productive activity of the intellect to a much greater degree than nature. This is evident if we consider that the activity of the intellect is more intense, more perfect, upon civilization than upon nature. Nature is imperfect civilization, because it will not clearly demonstrate the activity of the intellect of which it is a consequence. This is the reason for our impression of nature as something *prior to the intellect.* However, the progress of the natural sciences reveals, in an ever more evident way, the origin of nature in language.

We can now try to define the field of the *natural* sciences as opposed to the field of the sciences of *the spirit.* While the sciences of *the spirit* must research conversation in its depth, as a historical aspect, the *natural* sciences must study conversation in its breadth, as a current aspect. The sciences of *the spirit* are the study of conversation from the outside but into language, from thought to intellect; the *natural* sciences are the study of conversation from the inside but out of language, from intellect to thought. Fundamentally, both disciplines study the same reality: language. They are complementary disciplines.

The progress of the natural sciences has become vertiginous during the last generations. Nature changes rapidly and increases rapidly in extent. Simultaneously, the character of the concept *nature* becomes ever more evident. I remember the story told by Whitehead: *a shipwrecked scientist on a deserted island discovers a footprint in the sand. With his exact methods, he reconstructs the being that caused the footprint and discovers that he was this being himself.* This story is an illustration of the progress of the *natural* science. The intellectual and linguistic origin of *nature* is revealed by this progress. The phenomena of nature obey the rules of the language in which they are formulated. The mathematical and logical way nature behaves, which so impressed the scientists of the seventeenth and eighteenth centuries, is an evident consequence of the origin of nature in language.

Nature, as it has emerged in the territory of isolating languages, must be impenetrable to the methods of our *natural* science. From the point of view of these languages, our natural science must seem like magic. It is only when an isolating intellect apprehends and comprehends a fusional language, and therefore translates itself here, that it can participate in scientific conversation, that it can participate in our *nature*. What we can grasp of the isolating nature, without apprehending a language that corresponds to it, is very vague. However, we will have the impression that in the field of isolating languages, nature has the antistructural character of the language from which it emerged, as a set of isolating phenomena that forms an aesthetic whole. Nature is something to be lived, not comprehended. The very attempt to *comprehend* nature seems to be inconceivable to so-called Chinese *philosophers*. On the other hand, there is a developed discipline of the experience of nature that can be compared, vaguely, with our natural science. Lin Yutang, that great intellect who oscillates between the two territories, quotes a sage who says, *Westerners want to teach us their science and do not know how to stroll correctly.* I suspect, however, that Lin Yutang distorted Chinese thinking by translating it into English. The attempt to penetrate the isolating intellect to discover a parallel to our nature is bound, as always, to failure.

The difference between civilization and nature is therefore a difference of degree, not quality. Civilization is nature overcome; nature is potential civilization. But the process is reversible. Civilization can return to being nature, and the instruments of civilization can function, within the conversation, as phenomena of nature. How does this reversal occur? I believe this is a problem linked to the layers of language. Nature, of course, emerges in the layer of poetry. It is the poet who produces nature. Wilde's concept is well known: *nature is always more like Turner.* In the layer of conversation, nature is transformed into civilization and is thus expressed, expelled from the fabric of language. But poetic activity can seize this civilization; it can reincorporate it within language, and in this case, civilization becomes nature again. This process of reabsorption requires, as it seems to me, a special attention in our time, when we talk so much about the revolution of the machines that threaten to swallow us. The progress of the unconscious conversation of the poetic layer may very recently have been interpreted as the progressive struggle of the intellect against nature, transforming it into civilization. This interpretation is correct, provided we are not unaware that nature is provided to conversation by poetic activity. Of late, however, it seems to be civilization against which the intellect in conversation is called to fight. Civilization appears as a second-degree nature. The impression may arise that first-degree nature is exhausted and that conversation assumes this activity in a secondary degree. The sense of frustration, the existential *nausea,* that characterizes part of the present conversation and threatens to degenerate into small talk must have one of its causes in this interpretation of civilization and nature. Within this analysis, however, I believe that the problem dissolves. The creative activity of the intellect is free. It is not conditioned by *nature* (as the materialists of the eighteenth century thought) or by *civilization* (as nineteenth-century materialists thought) but develops within the norms of the language in which it thinks. The creative activity of the intellect is a product of the history of language, but a product that has overcome its historicity and has become free. It is therefore futile to want to analyze whether the proposals that poetry verts toward conversation are *natural* or *civilized*. If they are authentic, that is, if they come from the layer of poetry, they are elements of equal validity for the work of the intellect. By all means, the intellect can be realized, creating, in this process, reality—because nature per se and civilization per se are not real and become real only insofar as they are introduced or reintroduced into the conversation.

This discussion clarifies one more point. The sciences that deal with civilization, therefore, history (in the ordinary sense of that word), sociology, social anthropology, and so on, are natural sciences and have nothing in common with the sciences of the spirit (*Geisteswissenschaften*) as defined earlier. The phenomena studied by these sciences belong to the conversation in *breadth*, not in *depth*. There is, therefore, no ontological difference between this type of science and physics, for example. However, from this point of view, a hierarchy of the natural sciences emerges. We can establish an inclined plane along which *nature* slides toward *civilization*. This inclined plane will be the field of activity of the natural sciences. We can locate physics at its highest point, because it studies *nature* in its furthest form from *civilization* and closer to the verbal stage, and we can locate near the lowest point, for example, *art criticism*, because it studies *nature* in its most *civilized* form. What impresses in this inclined plane is the modification of the type of language that the different sciences will use, a modification proportional to the position of the respective science along the plane. Physics, for example, will be expressed in mathematical symbols, which will have no validity for art criticism (see chapter 3). Profoundly impressed by this modification of the language type of the sciences, Nicolai Hartmann uses the inclined plane as the starting point of an ontological analysis. He establishes *several layers of reality*. From *physical reality*, by mutation, an organic reality emerges, from this a spiritual reality, and so on. Each layer of reality participates in the lowest layer but contains something new and inexplicable from the lowest layer. The organic reality layer participates in physical reality, but it is not fully explicable in terms of physics. Although Hartmann's ontological analysis is fundamentally a linguistic analysis *(how to explicate, that is, articulate, reality?)*, he is not aware of that. What he teaches can be summarized as follows: the natural sciences (in the sense defined here) use different types of language, thus expressing different layers of reality. Hartmann would not agree with this summary, but I believe it to be valid nonetheless.

Within the ontological analysis of language undertaken in this work, Hartmann's position is unsustainable, although one must confess that Hartmann's concept of the layering is very fertile and certainly contributes to the formulation of the layers of language. I believe that the most fundamental of the divergences between Hartmann's analysis and this is the central position that the natural sciences occupy in Hartmann's system. Hartmann starts from the unconscious premise that the natural sciences research (and discover) the totality of reality. However, not being able to reconcile the various sciences with each other, owing to the intellectual honesty that characterizes him, Hartmann takes refuge in a reality hierarchized into layers. From the point of view of this analysis, however, the problem is different and subordinate. This is to explain the reason for the change in the type of language used by the natural sciences along the inclined plane. This explanation

stems organically from the analysis of language already undertaken: the language of physics is structurally the purest and has
symbols emptier than the language, for example, of art criticism,
because physics discusses phenomena upon which the intellect
in conversation acted less intensely, conversed less intensely. The
phenomena of physics, being more *natural* and less *civilized* than
the phenomena of art, make the (objective) *language* aspect more
evident and the (subjective) *intellect* aspect less so. They are closer
to *objective language* than to *subjective language*. As a result, the
language of physics is more evidently mathematical and formally
logical than the language of art criticism. But this is a difference of
quantity, not quality. In the course of conversation, the phenomena
of physics become art phenomena, because they are ontologically
identical. The difference in the type of language used by the natural sciences, therefore, has no ontological meaning, as Hartmann
thinks, but illustrates the progress of conversation from nature
toward civilization. It is interesting to note how the problem of
mathematics and pure logic reappears as a fundamental *layer,*
which was discussed in the previous chapter when it came to the
layer of oration. Logical symbolists, less honest than Hartmann,
stipulate the layer of mathematics as the background to which all
reality can be reduced. Hartmann teaches of the irreducibility of
reality onto a single layer. In contrast, symbolists have a much
deeper view of reality, which they recognize, implicitly or explicitly, as being identical to language. It is curious how a systematic
consideration of language always makes the same problems of
new angles reappear and encompasses them, putting them in
their respective places.

I ask the reader to return with me to the point of the argument
developed in this chapter, whose strands separated in somewhat
different directions, although always pointing to the same fundamental problem: language as a reality that grows in the course of
conversation, therefore language as a creative historical process.

Summarizing the threads and rearranging them into the thread of the argument, I can say this: *language, as projected from primitive babbling, has created nature, an ever-growing and ever-widening nature, and transformed that nature into civilization.* The creation of nature corresponds to the poetic activity of language, and the creation of civilization corresponds to the conversational activity of language, although this division is not strict. The so-called *natural* sciences, including those studying the phenomena of civilization, are researches of nature and civilization as they are being exposed, expressed, and articulated by current conversation; as they are currently being realized by this conversation. These sciences need to be supplemented, by introspective but no less rigorous disciplines, by the *sciences of the spirit* as proposed by Dilthey, that is, as studies of reality as the product of history. However, these new disciplines must be despsychologized, desubjectivized, as Husserl would have put it; in fact, they need to be developed according to the phenomenological method. This becomes possible, even organically necessary, as long as it is understood that *this reality as the product of history* is language as it becomes realized within each intellect currently in conversation. Therefore the science of the *spirit* has nothing psychological about it, being an introspective study of an objective phenomenon in the Husserlian sense. The intellect conceived as the product of the historical development of language is despsychologized and desubjectivized. It remains to be seen in what direction these new phenomenological disciplines, this new science of the *spirit,* can develop, in helping to complete the progress of the *natural* sciences.

I believe that a decisive step was taken by G. Misch, Dilthey's son-in-law and follower, in his book *Der Weg in die Philosophie,* expanded in the English translation as *The Dawn of Philosophy,* so as to include the author's thought until 1950. In this work, the concept of the *primordial word (Urwort)* is introduced.

Misch analyzes three civilizations, namely, the Western, Hindu, and Chinese civilizations, and comes to the conclusion that the thinking that characterizes each of them can be reduced to a primordial word proposed as the theme at the beginning of each civilization. In the case of the West, the word is *Logos*. In the case of India, the word is *Brahman*. In the case of China, the word is *Dao*. Of course, we cannot agree with Misch in his division of *civilizations*, nor do we have to agree with the primordial words he suggested. What is important in this type of speculation is a new (poetic) intuition of reality. What Misch teaches is that the conversations that make up reality (and what he calls civilizations) are variations and expansions, therefore, progressive realizations of an original theme, of a primordial word.

When we consult the conversation, of which we belong, about its origins, it does not respond, referring to its advance through the layers of babbling or the salad of words. This past of the conversation can be discovered only by research. The spontaneous answer that the conversation gives to our question is of an original inspiration from the unutterable. Conversation is believed to have been initiated by a creative act, expelled from nothingness by an articulation, an exclamation. This belief is common to all the conversations of which we are aware. The creative act, from which the conversation is believed to descend, is always a word. In the case of the Greek conversation, this primordial word is, as Misch shows, the word *word (Logos)*. In the case of Jewish conversation, this primordial word is the word *light*. When these two conversations were united, this primordial wisdom was expressed in the phrase *at the beginning was the Word*. Every conversation believes in its extralinguistic origin, believes it was created out of nothingness. It presupposes a poet *(poietés)* who articulated the whole conversation, proposing a word to be conversed. I believe that the sciences of the spirit, as defined here and such as Misch initiated, will, in this sense, be the search of the origin of language; they will be the search of the primordial word to come close to its poet. In this they will not be so different from the natural sciences, which are, in essence, looking for the same origin in the opposite direction. In this sense we can say that every scientific activity of the intellect, when authentic and quite radical, goes up to the layer of oration, both in the sense of peroration and in the sense of adoration. It looks for the horizons of language.

Before I leave this historical aspect of language, with its undiscussable origin from nothingness, I wish to draw attention once again to the tremendous beauty, the accumulated wisdom, of the majesty of language. Thus language spreads and spills toward us, through us, impelling us and impelled by us toward new conquests of reality. Each word, every grammatical form, is not only an accumulator of the whole past but also a generator of the whole future. Each word is a work of art projected into the reality of conversation from the unutterable, in whose refinement the countless generations of intellects in conversation have collaborated and which is entrusted to us by the conversation so that we may perfect it further and pass it on to those who will come, to serve it as instruments in their search for the unutterable. Which cathedral, symphony, or work of art can be compared in meaning, beauty, and wisdom with the word, any word, and from any language? To awaken this admiration, this humility, and this enthusiasm before the word will be the task of the science of the *spirit* as proposed here.

5

CONCLUSION

THE GREATER
CONVERSATION

The purpose of this work was to examine the proposition formulated and reformulated several times and whose most elaborate form is that language, that is, the set of symbol systems, is equal to the totality of what is apprehended and comprehended, that is, the totality of reality. The proposition starts from two definitions, formulated ad hoc, and which the reader must accept as definitions of terms if he or she wants to follow the development of the argument. The first is the definition of language as a set of symbol systems. The second is the definition of reality as that which can be apprehended and comprehended. This is, I repeat, a definition of terms, formulated ad hoc for the specific use of these two terms in the course of this investigation. If the conclusions we reach have any validity, it refers to the terms as defined earlier. However, this does not diminish its value in itself. Every discussion is a manipulation of terms, and its validity is restricted to these terms, as defined explicitly or implicitly.

Both terms were identified in the proposed proposition. Once the terms have been eliminated, the proposition can be formulated as follows: the set of symbol systems is equal to the totality of what can be apprehended and comprehended, or only symbols can be apprehended and comprehended. Formulated thus, the proposition reveals itself to be an ad hoc definition, namely, symbols are what can be apprehended and comprehended. This is a reversible definition, because it can be formulated thus: the apprehensible and comprehensible are symbols. Formally analyzed, this proposition is therefore purely tautological. What it says is, *if we define symbol as the apprehensible, and the apprehensible as symbol, since symbol is symbol, and the apprehensible is the apprehensible, then symbol is the apprehensible. And if we then define the set of symbols as language, and the set of the apprehensible as reality, then language is reality.* The reader will agree that the proposition thus formulated does not represent an especially happy effort by the intellect to formulate a new thought.

I suggest, however, that the logical analysis of the proposition, as I have applied it in the previous paragraph, has destroyed the poetic quality that possibly characterizes it in its dense form, namely, language is reality. I go further and suggest that any phrase, if analyzed logically, will sooner or later reveal its tautological character, losing in this process the poetic quality it may have possessed. I confess that it was such considerations that pushed me toward the investigation of language. I was struck by the creative power of poetic language and by the evaporation of that power under logical analysis, that is, by the logically analyzed tautology of language.

The proposition to be examined was proposed, therefore, in its most dense form, namely, language is reality, or there is no reality beyond language. As a consequence, the terms of the expanded proposition were not subjected to further analysis. *System, symbol, apprehend,* and *comprehend* are terms that have been employed constantly in this work, without having been clearly defined. This omission, if it is a mistake, is a deliberate error. I have fought, throughout the course of the argument, for a position that avoids the formalization and logicization of the problem, so as to avoid the sterilization of the problem. My purpose was not to arrive at logically unassailable positions and to establish a strictly consistent system: quite the opposite. I regard such positions and systems as meaningless and unproductive. My purpose was to subject the initial proposition to a process of internal conversation (what Plato calls *thought*) to ascertain how far it is fertile, to provoke new thoughts and broaden the conversation. I believe that it is a duty of intellectual honesty to openly declare the basic purpose of this work. Therefore I know this work will be subjected to the formal criticism that its numerous inaccuracies and failures will bring upon itself, should this work ever reach the conversation. However, the criticisms of thought, that is, the continuation of the argument, are what I really hope to awaken.

The process of internal conversation to which I have subjected the *poetic* proposition that has served as the theme of this work has revealed, as I had hoped, certain aspects of language that are not generally appreciated. It also provided insight into the whole of reality, in which certain problems are clarified, others are resolved, and others are dissolved. Finally, this internal conversation was a continuation of the great general conversation, which is now bifurcated in the subversion of formal philosophy and in the subversion of existential philosophy. By taking part in both of these subcontracts, it may, perhaps, serve as a bridge.

The Portuguese language is, among the highly developed languages that participate in the fusional conversation, one of the least philosophically *engaged*. I used it consciously, using it even as a plastic and malleable instrument. I must confess that my love for it is *that of the stranger who lives in its midst*. I have often replaced familiarity with intuition. I offer with gratitude this modest contribution to the Portuguese conversation, for what it is worth, and submit it to the punishments that my sins against the spirit of language will provoke.

With these final considerations, I want to plunge this work into the great river of conversation to be carried by the current of realization into the ocean of the unutterable.

Appendix

THE PHYSIOLOGY OF LANGUAGE

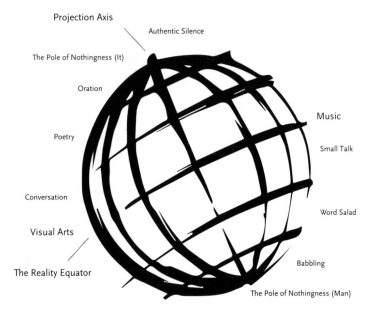

Projection Axis

Authentic Silence

The Pole of Nothingness (It)

Oration

Music

Poetry

Small Talk

Conversation

Word Salad

Visual Arts

The Reality Equator

Babbling

The Pole of Nothingness (Man)

Inauthentic Silence

LANGUAGE MAP

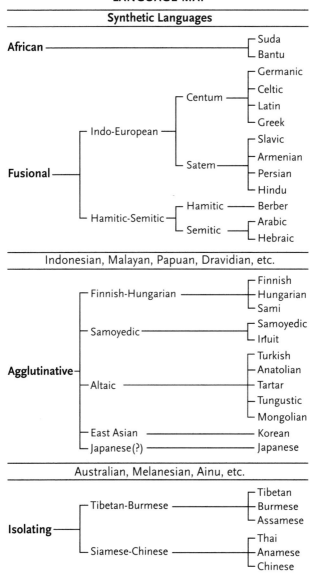

Synthetic Languages			

African —————————————————————— Suda / Bantu

Fusional — Indo-European — Centum — Germanic / Celtic / Latin / Greek

Satem — Slavic / Armenian / Persian / Hindu

Hamitic-Semitic — Hamitic — Berber

Semitic — Arabic / Hebraic

Indonesian, Malayan, Papuan, Dravidian, etc.

Agglutinative — Finnish-Hungarian — Finnish / Hungarian / Sami

Samoyedic — Samoyedic / Inuit

Altaic — Turkish / Anatolian / Tartar / Tungustic / Mongolian

East Asian — Korean

Japanese(?) — Japanese

Australian, Melanesian, Ainu, etc.

Isolating — Tibetan-Burmese — Tibetan / Burmese / Assamese

Siamese-Chinese — Thai / Anamese / Chinese

Bibliography

The following bibliography was originally published in the first edition of *Language and Reality* that Flusser wrote in Portuguese and published in 1963 in São Paulo. The significance of the source material from which Flusser drew part of his ideas should not go unnoticed to the interested reader. As any scholar of Flusser's work will note, although Flusser read almost indiscriminately, as widely as possible and in several languages, he rarely provided a list of his sources in his published works. As such, the bibliographical material presented here is a valuable scholarly resource for any researcher interested in Flusser's background and preparatory work.

Although the original bibliography was presented in a simplified format with only the surname of the author and the title, for the benefit of the reader of the present English-language edition, we have chosen to update the format to facilitate access and reference. Although the reader should keep in mind that Flusser's original list of bibliographic material contained a number of original English, German, or French editions, where an English-language translation of the French or German authors Flusser listed is now currently available, we have updated and provided this information for the benefit of the reader.

Chapter 1

Ammer, Karl. *Einführung in die Sprachwissenschaft.* Halle (Saale), Germany: Niemeyer, 1958.

Carnap, Rudolf. *The Logical Structure of the World and Pseudoproblems in Philosophy.* Chicago: Open Court, 2005.

Figueiredo, Cândido De. *Dicionário da língua portuguesa de Cândido de Figueiredo.* Lisbon: Bertrand, 1951.

Finck, Franz Nikolaus. *Die Haupttypen des Sprachbaus.* Darmstadt, Germany: Wissenschaftliche Buchgesellschaft, 1980.

Guardini, Romano. *Death of Socrates.* Cleveland, Ohio: World, 1948.

Herrigel, Eugen. *Zen in the Art of Archery.* New York: Vintage Books, 1999.

Hönigswald, Richard. *Philosophie und Sprache: Problemkritik und System.* Darmstadt, Germany: Wissenschaftliche Buchgesellschaft, 1970.

Jaensch, Erich Rudolf. *Die Natur der menschlichen Sprachlaute. Separatdruck aus: Zeitschrift für Sinnesphysiologie.* Leipzig, Germany: Barth, 1912.

Jensen, Hans. *Sign, Symbol, and Script: An Account of Man's Efforts to Write.* London: G. Allen and Unwin, 1970.

Jespersen, Otto. *Language: Its Nature, Development, and Origin.* N.p.: Hamlin Press, 2013.

Jünger, Ernst. *Geheimnisse der Sprache.* Frankfurt am Main, Germany: Vittorio Klostermann, 1963.

Jünger, Ernst. *Sprache und Körperbau.* Frankfurt am Main, Germany: Vittorio Klostermann, 1949.

Karlgren, Bernhard, and Bernhard Karlgren. *Sound and Symbol in Chinese.* Hong Kong: Hong Kong University Press, 1990.

Klages, Ludwig. *Die psychologischen Errungenschaften Nietzsches; Goethe als Seelenforscher; Die Sprache als Quell der Seelenkunde.* Bonn, Germany: Bouvier, 1980.

Koppers, Wilhelm. "Die Sprachfamilien und Sprachkreise der Erde." In *Festschrift P. W. Schmidt 76 sprachwissenschaftliche, ethnologische, religionswissenschaftliche, prähistorische und andere Studien*. Vienna: Mechitharisten-Congregations-Buchdruckerei, 1928.

Machado, José Pedro. *Dicionário etimológico da língua portuguesa*. Lisbon, 1956.

Mauthner, Fritz. *Beiträge zu einer Kritik der Sprache*. Leipzig, Germany: Felix Meiner, 1923.

Northrop, F. S. C. *The Meeting of East and West: An Inquiry Concerning World Understanding*. New York: Macmillan, 1946.

Pei, Mario A. *Encyclopedia of the Languages of the World*. London: Koros Press, 2011.

Révész, Géza, and Jay J. Butler. *The Origins and Prehistory of Language*. London: Longmans, Green, 1956.

Schlick, Moritz. *Allgemeine Erkenntnislehre*. Berlin: Springer, 2013.

Vossler, Karl. *Positivismus und Idealismus in der Sprachwissenschaft: Eine sprach-philosophische Untersuchung*. Heidelberg, Germany: C. Winter, 1904.

Weisgerber, Johann Leo. *Vom Weltbild der deutschen Sprache*. Dusseldorf, Germany: Padagogischer Verlag Schwann, 1953.

Wendt, Heinz F. *Das Fischer-Lexikon*. Frankfurt am Main, Germany: Fischer-Taschenbuch-Verlag, 1977.

Whitehead, Alfred North. *Modes of Thought*. New York: Free Press, 2010.

Whitehead, Alfred North. *Process and Reality*. New York: Free Press, 1978.

Chapter 2

Beauvoir, Simone De, and Constance Borde. *The Second Sex*. New York: Vintage Books, 2011.

Black, Max. *Language and Philosophy: Studies in Method*. Westport, Conn.: Greenwood Press, 1981.

Boodin, John. "Russell's Metaphysics." In *The Philosophy of Bertrand Russell,* edited by Paul Arthur Schilpp. La Salle, Ill.: Open Court, 1989.

Brunschvicg, Léon. *Héritage de mots: Héritage d'idées*. 2nd ed. Paris: PUF, 1950.

Camus, Albert. *The Fall*. Translated from the French by Justin O'Brien. London: Hamish Hamilton, 1957.

Camus, Albert. *The Myth of Sisyphus*. Translated from the French by Justin O'Brien. London: H. Hamilton, 1965.

Cassirer, Ernst. *Substance and Function; and, Einstein's Theory of Relativity*. Mineola, N.Y.: Dover, 2003.

Farber, Marvin. *The Foundation of Phenomenology: Edmund Husserl and the Quest for a Rigorous Science of Philosophy*. Frankfurt, Germany: Ontos, 2006.

Freud, Sigmund, Anna Freud, James Strachey, Alix Strachey, and Alan Tyson. *"The Ego and the Id": And Other Works*. London: Vintage and the Institute of Psycho-Analysis, 2001.

Hartmann, Eduard von, and Fritz Kern. *Kategorienlehre*. Leipzig, Germany: Meiner, 1923.

Hartmann, Nicolai. *Der Aufbau der realen Welt: Grundriss der allgemeinen Kategorienlehre*. Berlin: Walter de Gruyter, 1964.

Heidegger, Martin. *Being and Time*. Translated by Joan Stambaugh. Albany: State University of New York Press, 2010.

Heidegger, Martin, and David Farrell Krell. *Nietzsche*. London: Routledge and Kegan Paul, 1981.

Husserl, Edmund. *Introduction to Logic and Theory of Knowledge: Lectures 1906/07*. Translated by Claire Ortiz Hill. Dordrecht, Netherlands: Springer, 2008.

Husserl, Edmund. *Logical Investigations I*. Translated by J. N. Findlay. Edited by Dermot Moran. London: Routledge, 2001.

James, William. *Pragmatism, a New Name for Some Old Ways of Thinking: Together with Four Related Essays Selected from "The Meaning of Truth."* New York: Longmans, 1959.

James, William. *The Principles of Psychology*. New York: Dover, 1950.

Jaspers, Karl. *Philosophy of Existence*. Philadelphia: University of Pennsylvania Press, 1997.

Jaspers, Karl. *Vernunft und Existenz: Fünf Vorlesungen, gehalten vom 25. bis 29. März 1935*. Groningen, Germany: Wolters, 1935.

Kierkegaard, Søren. *Either/Or*. Garden City, N.Y.: Doubleday, 1959.

Marcel, Gabriel. *Being and Having*. Rochester, N.Y.: Scholars Choice, 2015.

Maritain, Jacques. *Existence and the Existent*. New York: Paulist Press, 2015.

Moore, G. E. *The Philosophy of G. E. Moore*. Edited by Paul Arthur Schilpp. La Salle, Ill.: Open Court, 1992.

Mounier, Emmanuel. *Existentialist Philosophies*. New York: Macmillan, 1949.

Nietzsche, Friedrich Wilhelm. *The Will to Power*. Translated by Walter Kaufmann. New York: Vintage Books, 1968.

Nietzsche, Friedrich Wilhelm, and Walter Arnold Kaufmann. *Thus Spoke Zarathustra: A Book for All and None*. New York: Penguin Books, 1987.

Sartre, Jean-Paul, and Lloyd Alexander. *Nausea: "The Wall" and Other Stories—Two Volumes in One*. New York: MJF Books, 1999.

Sartre, Jean-Paul, Mary Warnock, Hazel Estella Barnes, and Richard Eyre. *Being and Nothingness: An Essay on Phenomenological Ontology*. London: Routledge/Taylor and Francis, 2015.

Scholz, Heinrich, and Heti Gaertner. *Logistik: Vorlesung*. Munich, Germany: Mathematik Arbeitsgemeinschaft an der Universität, 1933.

Vaihinger, Hans. *Der Atheismusstreit gegen die Philosophie des Als Ob und das Kantische System*. Berlin: Reuther und Reichard, 1916.

Varet, Gilbert. "L'ontologie de Sartre." *Revue Philosophique de Louvain* 48, no. 18 (1950): 303.

Chapter 3

Bachofen, Johann Jakob. *Das Mutterrecht: Eine Untersuchung über die Gynaikokratie der alten Welt nach ihrer religiösen und rechtlichen Natur*. Frankfurt am Main, Germany: Suhrkamp, 2003.

Bell, Eric Temple. *The Development of Mathematics*. New York: Dover, 1992.

Bergson, Henri. *Creative Evolution*. Translated by Arthur Mitchell. Mineola, N.Y.: Dover, 1998.

Bergson, Henri, R. Ashley Audra, Cloudesley Brereton, and W. Horsfall

Carter. *The Two Sources of Morality and Religion.* Notre Dame, Ind.: University of Notre Dame Press, 2013.

Buber, Martin. *Dialogisches Leben: Gesammelte philosophische und päda-gogische Schriften.* Zurich, Switzerland: G. Müller, 1947.

Carnap, Rudolf. *Abriss der Logistik.* Berlin: Springer, 1929.

Carnap, Rudolf. *Meaning and Necessity.* Chicago: University of Chicago Press, 1967.

Cassirer, Ernst, Ralph Manheim, and Charles William Hendel. *The Philosophy of Symbolic Forms.* New Haven, Conn.: Yale University Press, 1998.

Dantzig, Tobias. *Number: The Language of Science.* New York: Plume, 2007.

Dewey, John. *Logic: The Theory of Inquiry.* N.p.: Read Books, 2008.

Frege, Gottlob. *Begriffsschrift, eine der arithmetischen nachgebildete Form-elsprache des reinen Denkens.* Halle, Germany: Verlag von Louis Nebert, 1879.

Godel, Kurt. *Mathematical Logic and Its Applications.* New York: Plenum Press, 1988.

Huxley, Julian. *Evolution: The Modern Synthesis.* Cambridge, Mass.: MIT Press, 2010.

Jaspers, Karl. *Philosophical Faith and Revelation.* London: Collins, 1967.

Jung, C. G. *The Symbolic Life: Miscellaneous Writings.* Vol. 18 of *Collected Works of C. G. Jung.* Translated by Gerhard Adler and R. F. C. Hull. Princeton, N.J.: Princeton University Press, 2014.

Kafka, Franz, and Breon Mitchell. *The Trial.* New York: Schocken Books, 1999.

Kierkegaard, Søren, and Alastair Hannay. *Fear and Trembling: Dialecti-cal Lyric by Johannes de Silentio.* London: Penguin Books, 2003.

Laird, John. *Recent Philosophy.* Freeport, N.Y.: Books for Libraries Press, 1973.

Lavelle, Louis. *La parole et lécriture.* Paris: Félin, 2005.

Lipps, Hans, and Evamaria Von Busse. *Die Verbindlichkeit der Sprache.* Frankfurt am Main, Germany: Vittorio Klostermann, 1977.

Malraux, André. *The Voices of Silence*. Princeton, N.J.: Princeton University Press, 2015.

Maritain, Jacques. *Creative Intuition in Art and Poetry*. New York: Pantheon Books, 1953.

Moore, George Edward. "Russell's Theory of Description." In *The Philosophy of Bertrand Russell*, edited by P. A. Schilpp, 177–225. La Salle, Ill.: Open Court, 1944.

Negley, Glenn. *The Organization of Knowledge: An Introduction to Philosophical Analysis*. Ann Arbor, Mich.: UMI, 1993.

Reichenbach, Hans. *Elements of Symbolic Logic*. New York: Dover, 1980.

Rickert, Heinrich. *Die Logik des Prädikats und das Problem der Ontologie*. Heidelberg, Germany: Carl Winter, 1930.

Russell, Bertrand. *An Inquiry into Meaning and Truth*. Nottingham, U.K.: Spokesman, 2007.

Russell, Bertrand. *The Analysis of Mind*. Whitefish, Mt.: Kessinger, 2010.

Vossler, Karl. *Geist und Kultur in der Sprache*. Munich, Germany: Dobbeck, 1960.

Waag, Albert. *Bedeutungsentwicklung unseres wortschatzes*. N.p.: Salzwasser, 2013.

Waismann, Friedrich. *Introduction to Mathematical Thinking: The Formation of Concepts in Modern Mathematics*. Translated by Theodore J. Benac. London: Hafner, 1952.

Weyl, Hermann. *Philosophy of Mathematics and Natural Science*. Princeton, N.J.: Princeton University Press, 2009.

Whitehead, Alfred North. *Principia mathematica*. Cambridge: Cambridge University Press, 1978.

Wittgenstein, Ludwig, and Charles Kay Ogden. *Tractatus logico-philosophicus*. London: Routledge, 2005.

Chapter 4

Bavink, Bernhard. *Das Weltbild der heutigen Naturwissenschaften und seine Beziehungen zu Philosophie und Religion*. Iserlohn, Germany: Silva, 1950.

Bridgman, P. W. *The Logic of Modern Physics*. Salem, N.H.: Ayer, 1993.

Broad, C. D. *Perception, Physics, and Reality: An Enquiry into the Information That Physical Science Can Supply about the Real*. Cambridge: Cambridge University Press, 1914.

Cassirer, Ernst. *The Problem of Knowledge: Philosophy, Science, and History since Hegel*. Translated by William H. Woglom. New Haven, Conn.: Yale University Press, 1978.

Croce, Benedetto. *La storia come pensiero e come azione*. Bari, Italy: Gius. Laterza e Figli, 1943.

Dilthey, Wilhelm. *The Formation of the Historical World in the Human Sciences*. Princeton, N.J.: Princeton University Press, 2002.

Dilthey, Wilhelm. *Introduction to the Human Sciences*. Princeton, N.J.: Princeton University Press, 1991.

Dilthey, Wilhelm, Stephen A. Emery, and William T. Emery. *The Essence of Philosophy*. New York: AMS Press, 1969.

Eddington, Arthur Stanley. *The Nature of the Physical World: Gifford Lectures of 1927*. Newcastle upon Tyne, U.K.: Cambridge Scholars, 2014.

Hartmann, Nicolai. *Möglichkeit und Wirklichkeit*. Berlin: Walter de Gruyter, 1966.

Hartmann, Nicolai. *Zur Grundlegung der Ontologie*. Berlin: Walter de Gruyter, 1965.

Heidegger, Martin, Julian Young, and Kenneth Haynes. *Off the Beaten Track*. Cambridge: Cambridge University Press, 2002.

Heisenberg, Werner. *Wandlungen in den Grundlagen der Naturwissenschaft*. Leipzig, Germany: S. Hirzel, 1947.

Husserl, Edmund. *Ideas Pertaining to a Pure Phenomenology and to a Phenomenological Philosophy*. Translated by Fred Kersten. Dordrecht, Netherlands: Kluwer, 2013.

Jaspers, Karl. *The Origin and Goal of History*. Translated by Michael Bullock. London: Routledge, 2010.

Jeans, James. *Physik und Philosophie*. Zurich, Switzerland: Rascher, 1944.

Kelsen, Hans. *Vergeltung und Kausalitat: Eine soziologische Untersuchung.* The Hague: W. P. van Stockun and Zoon, 1941.

Misch, Georg. *The Dawn of Philosophy: A Philosophical Primer.* London: Routledge and Kegan Paul, 1950.

Misch, Georg. *Lebensphilosophie und Phänomenologie.* Bonn, Germany: Cohen, 1929.

Schrödinger, Erwin. *Space–Time Structure.* Cambridge: Cambridge University Press, 1997.

Schrödinger, Erwin. *Uber Indeterminismus in der Physik: Its die Naturwissenschaft milieubedingt.* Leipzig, Germany: Verlag von Johann Ambrosius Barth, 1932.

Flusser Archive Collection

Post-History

Natural: Mind

The History of the Devil

On Doubt

Language and Reality

Foundational Concepts of Western Thought

Philosophy of Language

The Influence of Existential Thought Today

Vilém Flusser (1920–91) was born in Prague; emigrated to Brazil, where he taught philosophy and wrote a daily newspaper column; and later moved to France. Among his many books translated into English are *Does Writing Have a Future?*, *Into the Universe of Technical Images,* and *Writings,* all from Minnesota.

Rodrigo Maltez Novaes is an artist, researcher, translator, editor, and designer. He was a research fellow at the Vilém Flusser Archive from 2010 to 2014 and is a PhD candidate at the European Graduate School.